The Preaching of Pope Francis
Missionary Discipleship and the Ministry of the Word

Gregory Heille

D0103985

LITURGICAL PRESS
Collegeville, Minnesota

www.litpress.org

Cover design by Stefan Killen Design. Cover photo © *L'Osservatore Romano*.

1	2	3	4	5	6	7	8	9

Library of Congress Cataloging-in-Publication Data

Heille, Gregory, 1947–
   The preaching of Pope Francis : missionary discipleship and the ministry of the word / Gregory Heille.
      pages   cm
      ISBN 978-0-8146-4902-2 — ISBN 978-0-8146-4927-5 (ebook)
      1. Francis, Pope, 1936– 2. Catholic preaching.
   3. Witness bearing (Christianity)   I. Title.
   BX1378.7.H45   2015
   282.092—dc23   2014033119

"Fr. Gregory Heille's poetic and personal book is an act of love for a master preacher that convincingly shows how Pope Francis exemplifies all that the church has called for in the renewal of preaching. With considerable experience as a preacher and teacher of preaching, Fr. Heille links Pope Francis's homiletic practice with church documents on preaching in this beautiful, concise and heart-felt book."

—Deacon Peter Lovrick
Professor of Homiletics
St. Augustine's Seminary, Toronto

"Fr. Heille's book provides a broad frame by which the student-preacher can gain substantial insights into the missionary nuance of Pope Francis's preaching style. Both the new and experienced preacher will benefit from the way each chapter weaves together illustrations of Pope Francis's homilies with good preaching theory and method. The attentive selection, reading, and interpretation of the homilies that Fr. Heille offers highlight the depth and universality of Pope Francis's missionary discipleship. For those of us who may not readily label ourselves as preachers, the book gives us a rich meditation into the life of a pope who has captured our imagination."

—F. Javier Orozco
Executive Director of Intercultural and Interreligious
Affairs
Archdiocese of St. Louis

"Pope Francis places emphasis on preaching as a way to form missionary disciples. As a pastor I identified with Fr. Heille's point that: 'Daily preaching is a choral exercise of daily prayer supported by lifelong practices of discipleship, study, reflection, and service.' Proclaiming Good News to the poor is an essential part of the 'social dimension of Evangelization.'"

—Msgr. Charles Kosanke, Pastor, St. Regis Parish,
Bloomfield Hills, Michigan
Chairman, Catholic Charities of Southeast Michigan

To Fr. Paul Schumacher
who announced the resurrection to me
as a catechist in a grade-school cafeteria
one Wednesday evening in the Easter season
when I was sixteen.
That was the most important preaching I ever heard.

[W]e were gentle among you, as a nursing mother cares for her children. With such affection for you, we were determined to share with you not only the gospel of God, but our very selves as well, so dearly beloved had you become to us.

—1 Thessalonians 2:7-8

Contents

Prologue

Preaching and the Practice of Missionary Discipleship

Perhaps you have heard that it takes ten thousand hours to master a practice. Do you want to master painting, writing, running, prayer? Then give it ten thousand hours, and give it time every day. So, too, with the arts of ministry: do you want to be a counselor, a hospice chaplain, a church administrator, a pastor? Give it ten thousand hours and work at it every day.

Who do you know that has mastered the life practice of preaching? Do you think he or she has given it, say, three hours a day of preaching-related practices for ten years? That is what it takes.

Learning to preach takes much more effort than attending a few weekend workshops or a course at school. The preaching life is a practice, a way of life, and a way of discipleship. It is a whole-person commitment, and there is simply no one way to learn it or to do it or to master it. The authentic preaching life is a labor of love and a lifelong commitment.

Are you a preacher, or do you want to be? If so, what is your lifelong commitment, your practice, your labor of love, your preaching vocation? Be specific.

While relatively few of us in the church call ourselves preachers, all of us are nonetheless disciples. And Pope Francis reminds us that we all are called by virtue of our baptism and our missionary discipleship to testify to what we have heard and seen and touched in Christ. Christ is risen and alive and active in our midst—that is to say, in us, the people of God, the discipleship community. For this reason, each of us needs to ask from time to time what the ten-thousand-hour practice of discipleship looks like in our life.

Christianity is a vocation—to teaching, nursing, parenting, prayer, ministry, and ten thousand other things—and these ten thousand things constitute the reign of God and the beloved community of which the Scriptures and the church speak.

Pope Francis invites us to join Christianity's ten-thousand-hour club—to make a fundamental option for missionary discipleship and to take our lives to the foot of the cross and beyond, to the very peripheries of life where resurrection shines through. Pope Francis is speaking, and the whole of humanity is listening.

1
A Preacher as Pope

This is moving. Jesus, washing the feet of his disciples. Peter didn't understood it at all, he refused. But Jesus explained it for him. Jesus—God—did this! He himself explains to his disciples: "Do you know what I have done to you? You call me Teacher and Lord—and you are right, for that is what I am. So if I, your Lord and Teacher, have washed your feet, you also ought to wash one another's feet. For I have set you an example, that you also should do as I have done to you."

It is the Lord's example: he is the most important, and he washes feet, because with us what is highest must be at the service of others. This is a symbol, it is a sign, right? Washing feet means: "I am at your service." And with us too, don't we have to wash each other's feet day after day? But what does this mean? That all of us must help one another. Sometimes I am angry with someone or other . . . but . . . let it go, let it go, and if he or she asks you a favor, do it.

Help one another: this is what Jesus teaches us and this is what I am doing, and doing with all my heart, because it is my duty. As a priest and a bishop, I must be at your service. But it is a duty which comes from my heart: I love it. I love this and I love to do it because that is what the Lord has taught me to do. But you too, help one another: help one another always. One another. In this way, by helping one another, we will do some good.

Now we will perform this ceremony of washing feet, and let us think, let each one of us think: "Am I really willing, willing to serve, to help others?" Let us think about this, just this. And let us think that this sign is a

caress of Jesus, which Jesus gives, because this is the real
reason why Jesus came: to serve, to help us.

—Pope Francis, Mass of the Lord's Supper
Prison for Minors Casal del Marmo, Rome
Holy Thursday, 28 March 2013[1]

An Authentic Messenger

There is a "show me, don't tell me" quality to good preaching.
Part of this, of course, paradoxically has to do with the word-craft
of good rhetoric—engaging the listeners' imagination with images
that hit the metaphorical nail on the head by showing us what
the Good News looks like in our complex and messy real lives.

As we are seeing, Pope Francis is a master of metaphor,
and as a speaker he certainly captures the imagination of his
listeners. But of course, there is something more.

Many of us can readily recall how the new Bishop of Rome
captured our imagination on Holy Thursday a few days into
his pontificate. He preached a brief homily (only 311 words in
Italian) at Casal del Marmo, a youth prison in Rome. He told
his listeners very simply that Jesus' example of washing feet
is a symbol that says, "I am at your service." As he turned to
wash their feet, Pope Francis invited them to ask, "Am I really
willing to serve, to help others?"

Which do you remember—the 311 words of that homily,
or the image of this startling new pope washing the feet of
Muslim and Christian boys and girls in a youth prison on Holy
Thursday? We, the people of God throughout the world, were
the adults listening in on this children's homily. The pope was
preaching to us too, by example. We overheard, but we also
saw. And what did we see? We saw an essential message of
service, missionary discipleship, and the papacy.

After the Holy Thursday Mass of the Lord's Supper, a boy
asked, "Why did you come here today to Casal del Marmo?"
The pope replied, "It is a feeling that came from the heart."[2]

Good preaching is so heartfelt because it is so incarnational. A young cellist once commented that she loves the way

the vibration of her instrument strikes a vibration within the innermost recesses of her body. The body of the preacher is a stringed instrument, and as words play forth from the strings and sounding chambers of the body of the speaker, resonant chords are sounded upon the delicate structures of the ear and the incarnational intelligence of the listener. In the miracle of communication, heart speaks to heart.

When a remarkable catechist and Scripture scholar from Rome, Dr. Sofia Cavalletti, reflected on the relationship between adult and child in her book *The Religious Potential of the Child,* she wrote of the heart-to-heart communication between adult and child as a mutually enriching experience of "choral listening."[3] What begins in earliest childhood in the physical resonance of body communicating to body is always and essentially a soul communication.

Look, for example, at American painter Mary Cassatt's 1906 depiction of a young mother nursing her child, and see how mother and child are communicating through direct eye contact—and then consider that in his three-and-a-half-minute pre-conclave speech as one of the cardinal electors, Cardinal Borgoglio described the next pope as "someone who helps the Church surge forth to the peripheries like a sweet and comforting mother who offers the joy of Jesus to the world."[4] This image of comforting mother is one of his very favorite images.

A nursing mother once described the experience of breast-feeding her child as an experience of "prolonged conversation." As the church in its communities and its members humbly acknowledges that God speaks through dialogue and choral listening, perhaps we will give greater value to fostering the art of prolonged conversation. As the church becomes skilled in conversation, its preaching too will take on an aspect of listening and dialogue.

Listening and dialogue are often found at the edges of monologue-laden and noisy culture. By its liminality at the permeable boundaries and edges of culture, authentic exchange opens us to the transforming influence of God's Holy Spirit. In turn, renewed preaching, with its proclamation of Holy Scripture and in its reflective practice from the pulpit, will provide ritual focus and stimulus to the choral listening and dialogue of the entire community—even to the peripheries (to use another favorite expression of Pope Francis). Choral listening, in its many contexts and forms of dialogue, is the constitutive speech of a believing community.

In his apostolic exhortation *The Joy of the Gospel*, Pope Francis says that the Gospel is communicated in hearing and seeing and touch (29–31).[5] Gospel joy is communicated in the mutual transformation of hearing and speaking, seeing and showing, serving and accompanying. We, like the young people at Casal del Marmo, are called according to our baptism and our state of life to be reflective practitioners and proclaimers of the Gospel—missionary disciples and evangelists. And this missionary discipleship of service finds its authenticity in a choral listening of heart speaking to heart: *cor ad cor loquitor*.

By word and example, Pope Francis is a heartfelt reflective practitioner of the joy of the Gospel. In the authenticity of his day-to-day practice of the ministry, he also essentially and authentically communicates the pastoral heart of the Second Vatican Council and the council's intent to engage the modern world in dialogue. Theologians have been heard to say it can take a hundred years for an ecumenical council to make its impact. Halfway through this hundred-year arc of the most recent council's self-communication, Pope Francis lifts up Vatican II's pastoral torch by word and example as he calls and sends the people of God, by virtue of their baptism in Christ, as missionary disciples and evangelists (perhaps his most favorite expression).

A Day-to-Day Preacher

Whether at multiple Masses in a single parish or at multiple parishes—on Sundays and weekdays, at weddings and funerals and quinceañeras, and in schools and nursing homes—Catholic priests today not uncommonly preach a thousand times per year. Thank God, there are deacons and, in some settings, lay ecclesial ministers to share the responsibility of proclaiming the Word. And thank God, too, that the cardinal electors have given us a preacher pope—a seasoned daily minister of the Word who knows what it means to sustain the nourishing discipline of daily preaching.

On most days, Pope Francis presides and preaches at daily Mass in the chapel that seats fifty at Domus Sanctae Marthae—the Vatican guest hotel in which from the beginning he has taken residence. His unscripted remarks are brief, closely tied to the Scriptures and the feasts and cycles of the liturgical year, and they are laced with imagery and metaphors that speak to faith, life, and current events. His daily homilies are unguarded, transparent, and often prophetic. And interestingly, while brief daily summaries are posted online by the Vatican[6] and are closely followed by many bishops and clergy and laity alike, most often these homilies cannot be found in print—which seems to be just as the pope has intended it.

These little homilies are newsworthy and of great interest, yet the pope appears to understand the ephemeral nature of daily preaching. For both preacher and listener alike, daily preaching is an exercise in daily prayer and meditation—most often an unscripted engagement with the daily portion of the liturgy and with personal and communal and global events. Daily preaching is a choral exercise of daily prayer supported by lifelong practices of discipleship, study, reflection, and service. Daily preaching is best as unguarded speech, given in a communal circle of vulnerability and trust—open to life's questions and sufferings and open to unexpected daily events and the promptings of the Holy Spirit. These words of countless daily homilies are not meant to be written down or even long remembered. Rather, they are a daily portion in the choral listening of a liturgical assembly turning its collective ear to God, who as the living Word is alive and active every day and for each moment, *cor ad cor loquitor.*

As busy pastors grapple to come to terms with a sustainable practice of day-in, day-out preaching, St. Augustine's citation of the orator Cicero comes to mind:

> An eloquent man once said . . . and what he said was true,
> that to be eloquent you should speak "so as to teach, to
> delight, to sway." Then he added, "Teaching your audience
> is a matter of necessity, delighting them a matter of being
> agreeable, swaying them a matter of victory." Of these
> three, the one put first, that is the necessity of teaching,
> is to be found in the things we are saying, the remaining
> two in the way we say it. Therefore the person who is say-
> ing something with the intention of teaching should not
> consider he has yet said anything of what he wants to the
> person he wishes to teach, so long as he is not understood.
> Because even if he has said something he understands him-
> self, he is not to be regarded as having said it to the person
> he is not understood by, while if he has been understood,
> he has said it, whatever his way of saying it may have been.
>
> If on the other hand he also wishes to delight the per-
> son he is saying it to, or to sway him, he will not succeed
> in doing so whatever his way of saying it may have been;
> but in order to do so, it makes all the difference how he
> says it. Now just as the listener needs to be delighted if
> you are to hold his attention and keep him listening, so
> he needs to be swayed, if you are to move him to act.[7]

Daily preaching, to be sustained well by the preacher and
by an assembly of listeners, must teach, delight, and persuade.
A well-ordered palette of daily teaching tends over the long
haul to interpret life and mediate meaning through the Scriptures (exegesis and hermeneutics), to interpret life and mediate
meaning through the seasons, prayers, music, and symbols and
gestures of the liturgy (mystagogy), and to interpret life and
mediate meaning through such great theological themes as the
Trinity or the paschal mystery (orthodoxy) and through group
spiritual direction in Christian discipleship (orthopraxis). Pope
Francis tends to all of these.

Sustainable daily preaching also takes delight in the authentic support found in the context of a loving, compassionate,
and encouraging community and pastor. People respond joy-
fully and gratefully to a pastor who prayerfully enters into the
liturgy, choosing prayers and making connections to support

a simple and direct Gospel message. A daily preaching that explores one point for a few minutes without many or any notes—gratefully and delightfully—can be plenty good enough.

The continuity of daily preaching can be very persuasive—as preacher and assembly together discover a weekly narrative of Old and New Testament readings, seasons and feasts, and personal and public events. In some measure, daily communicants are seeking a safe place to regulate daily stress and to ground their discipleship in reflection and right living.

Pope Francis is a day-to-day icon of "to teach, to delight, to persuade." What we observe him doing each day in his Santa Marthae worshipping community plays out likewise in our experience of daily churches and chapels around the world. Day by day, faith communities are sustained as the church by Christ in word and sacrament. And day by day, we in turn as the Body of Christ sustain our families, our workplaces, and our world. We, too, are, as Pope Francis tells us, missionary disciples and evangelists. We, too, are called and sent to teach, to delight, and to persuade.

At the Pastoral Peripheries

Pope Francis feels drawn to the "peripheries." This Argentinian bishop of the slums likes to eat in the cafeteria line and preach in prisons, and he likes to pick up the telephone or go to the back of the airplane for an interview. He is a pastor who wants to be with the folks, and he likes having friends in low places.

For Pope Francis, being Bishop of Rome means saying his daily Mass with his day-to-day worshipping community at the Vatican hotel, and it also means going outside the walls to visit the parishes of Rome. Each month when possible, he tries to make a pastoral visit to one of the parishes, presiding and preaching at a Sunday Eucharist. These preachings, posted in their entirety in multiple languages at the Vatican website, present us with a monthly snapshot of Pope Francis as a pastoral preacher to ordinary folk who most certainly live their lives outside the ecclesiastical perimeter of the Vatican.

These Sunday homilies range from seven- to eight-hundred words (one single-spaced page) and preach from seven to eight minutes. Pope Francis refrains from using these occasions as a soapbox for larger ecclesiastical or social issues. He likes to start directly from one of the Scriptures, paint a mental picture of Jesus, and ask questions—questions that engage a dialogue with the lives of ordinary parishioners.

Here, for example, is the first half of a homily that led into the confirmation of youngsters at St. Cyril of Alexandria Parish in Rome:

> In the First Reading we heard the Prophet Isaiah speak to us about a journey, and he says that in the latter days, at the end of the journey, the mountain of the Lord's Temple shall be established as the highest mountain. He says this to tell us that our life is a journey: we must go on this journey to arrive at the mountain of the Lord, to encounter Jesus. The most important thing that can happen to a person is to meet Jesus: this encounter with Jesus who loves us, who has saved us, who has given his life for us. Encounter Jesus. And we are journeying in order to meet Jesus.
>
> We could ask ourselves this question: But when do I meet Jesus? Only at the end? No, no! We meet him every day. How? In prayer, when you pray, you meet Jesus. When you receive Communion, you meet Jesus in the Sacraments. When you bring your child to be baptized, you meet Jesus, you find Jesus. And today, you who are receiving Confirmation, you too will encounter Jesus; then you will meet him in Communion. "And then, Father, after Confirmation, goodbye?" because they say that Confirmation is called "the sacrament of goodbye." Is this true or not? After Confirmation you never go back to Church: true or false? . . . so, so! However, after Confirmation even, our whole life is an encounter with Jesus: in prayer, when we go to Mass, and when we do good works, when we visit the sick, when we help the poor, when we think of others, when we are not selfish, when we are loving . . . in these things we always meet Jesus. And the journey of life is precisely this: journeying in order to meet Jesus.[8]

Pope Francis likes to keep his hand in as a priest and pastor. In the first half of his homily in a pastoral visit to San Tommaso Apostolo Parish in Rome, he preached similarly in what is becoming his familiar pastoral preaching style—a style laced with scriptural imagery, the inner struggles of life, and a line of questioning that enters into dialogue with real life and points to the more engaged discipleship:

> One time, the disciples of Jesus were eating grain because they were hungry; but it was Saturday and on Saturday grain was not allowed to be eaten. Still, they picked it [rubbing his hands together] and ate the grain. And they [the Pharisees] said: "But look at what they are doing! Whoever does this breaks the Law and soils his soul, for he does not obey the Law!" And Jesus responded: "nothing that comes from without soils the soul. Only what comes from within, from your heart, can soil your soul." And I believe that it would do us good today to think not about whether my soul is clean or dirty, but rather about what is in my heart, what do I have inside, what I know I have but no one else knows. Being honest with yourself is not easy! Because we always try to cover it up when we see something wrong inside, no? So that it doesn't come out, don't we? What is in our heart: is it love? Let us think: do I love my parents, my children, my wife, my husband, people in the [neighborhood], the sick? . . . Do I love? Is there hate? Do I hate someone? Often we find hatred, don't we? "I love everyone except for this one, this one and that one!" That's hatred, isn't it? What is in my heart, forgiveness? Is there an attitude of forgiveness for those who have offended me, or is there an attitude of revenge—"he will pay for it!" We must ask ourselves what is within, because what is inside comes out and harms, if it is evil; and if it is good, it comes out and does good. And it is so beautiful to tell ourselves the truth, and feel ashamed when we are in a situation that is not what God wants, it is not good; when my heart feels hatred, revenge, so many situations are sinful. How is my heart?[9]

Oriented to Service and Evangelization

In February 2013, when Pope Benedict XVI announced his intention to resign the papacy, he clearly intended for a new pope to have the world stage during the upcoming Holy Week. Shortly thereafter, in his three-and-a-half-minute speech to the papal electors prior to the conclave, Cardinal Jorge Mario Borgoglio said that the church is "too self-referential."[10] And from the moment he stepped onto the papal balcony on the evening of his election, he communicated a demeanor that said, "This is not about me."

Six days after his election, at the Mass on the occasion of the inauguration of his pontificate, Francis preached on the true meaning of power:

> Today, together with the feast of Saint Joseph, we are cele-brating the beginning of the ministry of the new Bishop of Rome, the Successor of Peter, which also involves a certain power. Certainly, Jesus Christ conferred power upon Peter, but what sort of power was it? Jesus' three questions to Peter about love are followed by three commands: feed my lambs, feed my sheep. Let us never forget that authentic power is service, and that the Pope too, when exercising power, must enter ever more fully into that service which has its radiant culmination on the Cross. He must be inspired by the lowly, concrete and faithful service which marked Saint Joseph and, like him, he must open his arms to protect all of God's people and embrace with tender affection the whole of humanity, especially the poorest, the weakest, the least important, those whom Matthew lists in the final judgment on love: the hungry, the thirsty, the stranger, the naked, the sick and those in prison (cf. Mt 25:31-46). Only those who serve with love are able to protect![11]

At his first chrism Mass, Pope Francis spoke to priests about a preaching ministry that takes them to the peripheries—and as with his preaching to the imprisoned youth at Casal del Marmo later that evening, we the people of God were listening in to an important message about vocation to the practice of service:

The priest who seldom goes out of himself, who anoints
little—I won't say "not at all" because, thank God, the
people take the oil from us anyway—misses out on the
best of our people, on what can stir the depths of his
priestly heart. Those who do not go out of themselves,
instead of being mediators, gradually become intermediar-
ies, managers. We know the difference: the intermediary,
the manager, "has already received his reward," and since
he doesn't put his own skin and his own heart on the line,
he never hears a warm, heartfelt word of thanks. This is
precisely the reason for the dissatisfaction of some, who
end up sad—sad priests—in some sense becoming collec-
tors of antiques or novelties, instead of being shepherds
living with "the [odor] of the sheep." This I ask you: be
shepherds, with the "[odor] of the sheep," make it real, as
shepherds among your flock, fishers of men. True enough,
the so-called crisis of priestly identity threatens us all and
adds to the broader cultural crisis; but if we can resist its
onslaught, we will be able to put out in the name of the
Lord and cast our nets. It is not a bad thing that reality
itself forces us to "put out into the deep," where what we
are by grace is clearly seen as pure grace, out into the deep
of the contemporary world, where the only thing that
counts is "unction"—not function—and the nets which
overflow with fish are those cast solely in the name of the
One in whom we have put our trust: Jesus.[12]

That Saturday at the Easter Vigil, Pope Francis assumed the
pastoral, dialogical style seen in his monthly pastoral visits to
parishes in Rome. A pope of surprises spoke about a God of
surprises, making it clear that like the women at the tomb of
Jesus, we, too, are called to encounter Jesus and to proclaim
resurrection:

In the Gospel of this radiant night of the Easter Vigil,
we first meet the women who go to the tomb of Jesus
with spices to anoint his body (cf. Lk 24:1-3). . . . We
can imagine their feelings as they make their way to the
tomb: a certain sadness, sorrow that Jesus had left them,
he had died, his life had come to an end. Life would now

go on as before. Yet the women continued to feel love, the love for Jesus which now led them to his tomb. But at this point, something completely new and unexpected happens, something which upsets their hearts and their plans, something which will upset their whole life: they see the stone removed from before the tomb, they draw near and they do not find the Lord's body. It is an event which leaves them perplexed, hesitant, full of questions: "What happened?," "What is the meaning of all this?" (cf. Lk 24:4). Doesn't the same thing also happen to us when something completely new occurs in our everyday life? We stop short, we don't understand, we don't know what to do. Newness often makes us fearful, including the newness which God brings us, the newness which God asks of us. We are like the Apostles in the Gospel: often we would prefer to hold on to our own security, to stand in front of a tomb, to think about someone who has died, someone who ultimately lives on only as a memory. . . . [W]e are afraid of God's surprises! He always surprises us! The Lord is like that.

. . . And the two men in dazzling clothes tell them something of crucial importance: remember. "Remember what he told you when he was still in Galilee. . . ." This is the invitation to remember their encounter with Jesus, to remember his words, his actions, his life; and it is precisely this loving remembrance of their experience with the Master that enables the women to master their fear and to bring the message of the Resurrection to the Apostles and all the others (cf. Lk 24:9).[13]

This same invitation to all the faithful to encounter Jesus and to light a fire of resurrection faith for all the world is repeated forcibly and passionately a year later by Pope Francis at his second Easter Vigil: "For each of us, too, there is a 'Galilee' at the origin of our journey with Jesus. 'To go to Galilee' means something beautiful, it means rediscovering our baptism as a living fountainhead, drawing new energy from the sources of our faith and our Christian experience. To return to Galilee means above all to return to that blazing light with which

God's grace touched me at the start of the journey. From that flame I can light a fire for today and every day, and bring heat and light to my brothers and sisters."[14]

And fifty days later, on Pentecost, Pope Francis asserted that this baptism we share with the church is a baptism of the Holy Spirit that is born in going out to proclaim the Good News at the peripheries:

> This remembrance in the Spirit and by virtue of the Spirit is not reduced to a mnemonic fact; it is an essential aspect of Christ's presence within us and within his Church. The Spirit of truth and charity reminds us of all that Christ said, and helps us to enter ever more fully into the meaning of his words. We all have this experience: one moment, in any situation, there is an idea and then another connects with a passage from Scripture. . . . It is the Spirit who leads us to take this path: the path of the living memory of the Church. And he asks us for a response: the more generous our response, the more Jesus' words become life within us, becoming attitudes, choices, actions, testimony. In essence the Spirit reminds of the commandment of love, and calls us to live it. . . .
>
> The day of Pentecost, when the disciples "were all filled with the Holy Spirit," was the baptism of the Church, which was born in "going out," in "departure" to proclaim the Good News to everyone. The Mother Church, who departs in order to serve. Let us remember the other Mother, our Mother who sets out in haste to serve. Mother Church and Mother Mary: both virgins, both mothers, both women. Jesus was peremptory with the Apostles: do not depart from Jerusalem, but wait until you have received the power of the Holy Spirit from above (cf. Acts 1:4-8). Without Him there is no mission, there is no evangelization. For this, with the whole Church, with our Mother Catholic Church, let us implore: Come, Holy Spirit![15]

A Homiletic Magisterium

Pope Francis's magisterial teaching about our baptismal call to be missionary disciples at the peripheries is grounded every day in the authenticity of his preaching, both with and without words. The message, style, and contexts of his daily example and preaching are themselves an instruction in discipleship. The simplicity and relevancy of this daily message mediate meaning, and this cumulative overflow of daily meaning might be called Pope Francis's quotidian magisterium—an ordinary-time kind of teaching with day-in, day-out pastoral and doctrinal authority. The authenticity of Pope Francis's message reaches well beyond the walls of Vatican City to ordinary Catholics everywhere, and beyond Catholicism to believers and to people of goodwill everywhere. Pope Francis has captured the world's imagination with a meaningful message that conveys the joy of the Gospel.

As can be seen further in a close reading of his apostolic exhortation of that same name—*Evangelii Gaudium* (The Joy of the Gospel)—Pope Francis, in the formal documents of his teaching office, likewise makes his consistent appeal to Christians in every station and circumstance of life: we are being called by virtue of our faith and baptism to be missionary disciples, and we are being sent to the peripheries as evangelists to testify with our lives to the joy of the Gospel.

This core message of the Bishop of Rome from the Argentinian periphery was conveyed beautifully in his weekly *Angelus* message in St. Peter's Square on January 6, 2014, the Solemnity of the Epiphany of the Lord. These short weekly messages are homilies in themselves, and unlike his daily preaching at Domus Sanctae Marthae, these weekly messages are printed in full at the Vatican website. In his Epiphany message, Pope Francis said:

> Thus, this Feast lets us see a double movement: in one direction, the movement of God towards the world, towards humanity—the whole of the history of salvation, which culminates in Jesus—and in the other, the movement of men towards God—let us think of religions, of the quest for truth, the journey of the nations toward peace, interior peace, justice, freedom. And this double movement is driven by a mutual attraction. What is it that draws

God? . . . The Prophet Isaiah said that God is like the flower of the almond tree. Why? Because in that region the almond is the first to flower. And God goes ever before, he is always the first to seek us, he takes the first step. God goes ever before us. His grace precedes us and this grace appeared in Jesus. He is the Epiphany. He, Jesus Christ, is the manifestation of God's love. He is with us.

The Church stands entirely within this movement of God toward the world: her joy is the Gospel, to mirror the light of Christ. The Church is the people who have experienced this attraction and bear it within, in their hearts and in their lives. I would like to say—sincerely—I would like to say to those who feel far from God and from the Church—I would like to say respectively—to all those who are fearful or indifferent: the Lord is also calling you to be a part of his people and he does so with deep respect and love! . . .

Let us ask God, on behalf of the whole Church, let us ask for the joy of evangelizing, for we were "sent by Christ to reveal and communicate the love of God to all men and to all peoples." May the Virgin Mary help us all to be missionary-disciples, little stars that mirror his light. Let us pray too that hearts be open to receiving the proclamation, and that all men and women may be "partakers of the promise in Christ Jesus through the Gospel" (Eph 3:6).[16]

2

You Cannot Imprison the Word of the Lord

Those who have opened their hearts to God's love, heard his voice and received his light, cannot keep this gift to themselves. Since faith is hearing and seeing, it is also handed on as word and light. Addressing the Corinthians, Saint Paul used these two very images. On the one hand he says: "But just as we have the same spirit of faith that is in accordance with scripture—'I believed, and so I spoke'—we also believe, and so we speak" (2 Cor 4:13). The word, once accepted, becomes a response, a confession of faith, which spreads to others and invites them to believe. Paul also uses the image of light: "All of us, with unveiled faces, seeing the glory of the Lord as though reflected in a mirror, are being transformed into the same image" (2 Cor 3:18). . . . The light of Christ shines, as in a mirror, upon the face of Christians; as it spreads, it comes down to us, so that we too can share in that vision and reflect that light to others, in the same way that, in the Easter liturgy, the light of the paschal candle lights countless other candles. Faith is passed on, we might say, by contact, from one person to another, just as one candle is lighted from another. (37)

—Pope Francis, *Lumen Fidei*[1]

Church for the Modern World

For purposes of understanding the ministry of the Word through the lens of Pope Francis, it may be useful to think back through what might be defined as three eras of Christendom, beginning with Constantine and the age of the institution, continuing with the Enlightenment and the age of the individual, and presently moving—we may hope—toward an age of community. Each age demonstrates a different preferential option—for the aristocracy, for the middle class, and for the poor. Under this schema, each age can be characterized using a number of different descriptors:

Age of the Institution	Age of the Individual	Age of Community
Option for the Aristocracy	Option for Middle Class	Option for the Poor
Consistency	Progress	Process
Faith	Reason	Reflection
Transcendence	Imminence	Coherence
Spirit	Matter	Body
Control	Freedom	Responsibility
Doctrine	Science	Praxis
Empire	Nation States	Cities
Reign	Management	Governance
Authority and Obedience	Independence	Interdependence
Head and Members	Parts	System
Organism	Machine	Hologram
Patron and Client	Workers	Citizens
Law	Competition	Engagement
Mandate	Debate	Dialogue
Domination	Isolation	Participation
Exclusion	Polarization	Inclusion
Crusade	War	Nonviolence
Conquest	Struggle	Liberation
Sacrifice	Defense	Resistance

Though these lists speak in terms of three ages corresponding to the gestalt of a chronological period in history, it is equally true to think of them as three mindsets or value systems or modes of operation concurrently held by different institutions, persons, and communities in our age—often at cross purposes. As each new paradigm of social organization arises, its plausibility is in large measure determined by its critique of the other paradigms that have preceded it, but its viability may be determined by its ability to coexist with those same differing paradigms.

If a new paradigm of social organization is manifesting itself over the long arc of the Second Vatican Council church—the diverse mindsets and hopes of both papal electors and rank-and-file Catholics notwithstanding—it is because we as church are in an arc of postmodern crisis. As we face the ecclesiastical crises of philosophical relativism, theological ignorance, pastoral abuse, institutional mismanagement, and congregational malaise, we may instinctively try to patch our messy church together with the familiar institutional and individualistic approaches of the past. But public opinion doesn't seem to think we are succeeding. We badly need to reframe our self-understanding and modes of practice as church, and old paradigms are not always proving equal to the task.

The communitarian paradigm is not emerging *ex nihilo*. It is, rather, a theological product of the inculturation between the Gospel and the cultures of the poor. In Argentina, Jorge Borgoglio, SJ, lived at this nexus of inculturation. As a young Jesuit provincial, he tried relatively unsuccessfully to manage his responsibilities from an institutional paradigm. But the human suffering suffered by priests and people at the hands of a military regime pointed Borgoglio to the peripheries. And there in the barrios, he found Gospel authenticity in the pastoral spirit of Vatican II—specifically, a Gospel solidarity in a modern world laced with joy and hope, as well as with grief and anguish. In the words of Vatican II's *Gaudium et Spes*:

> The joys and the hopes, the griefs and anguish of the
> people of our time, especially those who are poor or af-

flicted, are the joys and hopes, the grief and anguish of
the followers of Christ as well. Nothing that is genuinely
human fails to find an echo in their hearts. For theirs is a
community of people united in Christ and guided by the
Holy Spirit in their pilgrimage to the Father's kingdom,
bearers of a message of salvation for all humanity. That
is why they cherish a feeling of deep solidarity with the
human race and its history.

Now that the Second Vatican Council has studied the
mystery of the Church more deeply, it addresses not only
the daughters and sons of the church and all who call upon
the name of Christ, but the whole of humanity as well,
and it wishes to set down how it understands the presence
and function of the church in the world of today (1–2).[2]

Pope Francis is a Vatican II leader inviting us to the peripheries. Like Christ and St. Francis and so many others, Pope
Francis invites us to make a fundamental option for the poor.
Time and time again, he models in his speech and in his behav-
ior the paradigm, not of the institution or of the individual, but
of community. The whole story of Vatican II and its ensuing
papacies could be told as a journey in fits and starts to this new
communal destination.

In his encyclical letter *Lumen Fidei* (The Light of Faith),
Francis speaks of "The Ecclesial Form of Faith":

In this way, the life of the believer becomes an ecclesial existence, a life lived in the Church. . . . And just as
Christ gathers to himself all those who believe and makes
them his body, so the Christian comes to see himself as a
member of this body, in an essential relationship with all
other believers. The image of a body does not imply that
the believer is simply one part of an anonymous whole,
a mere cog in a great machine; rather, it brings out the
vital union of Christ with believers and of believers among
themselves (cf. Rom 12:4-5). Christians are "one" (cf.
Gal 3:28), yet in a way which does not make them lose
their individuality; in service to others, they come into
their own in the highest degree. This explains why, apart
from this body, outside this unity of the Church in Christ,

outside this Church which—in the words of Romano Guardini—"is the bearer within history of the plenary gaze of Christ on the world"—faith loses its "measure"; it no longer finds its equilibrium, the space needed to sustain itself. Faith is necessarily ecclesial; it is professed from within the body of Christ as a concrete communion of believers. It is against this ecclesial backdrop that faith opens the individual Christian towards all others. Christ's word, once heard, by virtue of its inner power at work in the heart of the Christian, becomes a response, a spoken word, a profession of faith. As Saint Paul puts it: "one believes with the heart . . . and confesses with the lips" (Rom 10:10). Faith is not a private matter, a completely individualistic notion or a personal opinion: it comes from hearing, and it is meant to find expression in words and to be proclaimed. For "how are they to believe in him of whom they have never heard? And how are they to hear without a preacher?" (Rom 10:14). Faith becomes operative in the Christian on the basis of the gift received, the love which attracts our hearts to Christ (cf. Gal 5:6), and enables us to become part of the Church's great pilgrimage through history until the end of the world. For those who have been transformed in this way, a new way of seeing opens up, faith becomes light for their eyes. (22)

A Church Called to Reflective Practice

When church people resort through force of habit or indeliberate ignorance and pathological fear to the controlling and polarizing behaviors characteristic of the shadow side of institutionalism and individualism, people suffer injury. The alternative requires a move to second-order change—characterized by reflection, dialogue, inclusion, participation, and nonviolence.

In *Lumen Fidei*, Pope Francis states that "Christian faith, inasmuch as it proclaims the truth of God's total love and opens us to the power of that love, penetrates to the core of our human experience" (32). And *penetrating to the heart of human experience with the eyes of faith* is a fairly neat definition of the process of theological reflection.

In the 1990s, thirty years into the arc of implementation of Vatican II, James D. Whitehead and Evelyn Eaton Whitehead wrote *Method in Ministry: Theological Reflection and Christian Ministry*, in which they made a case that theological reflection is commensurate with the full, conscious, and active participation of the baptized faithful envisioned by Vatican II. They said that this process of reflection is engaged by instigating a conversation among three sources of religiously relevant information—the experience of the community of faith, the Christian tradition, and the resources of the surrounding culture.[3] This second-order, reflective conversation always is with a view to social and theological analysis and strategic action.

The Christian art of theological reflection is an art of dialogue—of prolonged conversations between persons, of faith-filled reflections within the discipleship community, and of mutually transforming encounters of believing communities and their component cultures. Each partner to dialogue brings the perspective of experience, most especially the experience of what has been heard and seen and touched in Christ.

A twentieth-century pioneer in theological reflection, Fr. Joseph Cardijn, in Belgium in the years surrounding World War I, founded the Young Christian Workers (YCW) with the desire to lead young workers into deeper appropriation of faith through a see-judge-act model of faith reflection on experience—what the Whiteheads call a process of attending, assertion, and pastoral response. The process invites the participant to see or observe experience without interpretation—to narrate the who, what, where, and when of experience without leaping to the interpretative why. This is a very difficult skill for most people to learn—the temptation is to leap to judgment. Theological reflection refuses to make this leap too quickly; rather, we are encouraged first to step back, to observe. Only then do we engage the second step of the see-judge-act process: in which we as participants in the process then judge or interpret our experience through an evaluative assessment in light of core Christian teaching, virtues, and social practices. We do not leap to judgment; rather, we make a more detached and considered judgment in light of our faith. And this process, in turn, always is intended to result in positive action or transformative practice: see-judge-act. This reflective process that we call theological reflection might be defined as *an action-oriented, faith- and value-driven, graced and messy dialogue with experience.*

What began with the YCW grew also into two other movements—Young Christian Students (YCS) and the Christian Family Movement (CFM)—making a strong mark in Europe, the United States, and elsewhere on the pre-council appropriation of faith by the laity in the 1950s. The movement later was affirmed by Cardijn's consecration as bishop by Cardinal Joseph Suenens and Cardijn's elevation as a cardinal by Pope Paul VI in 1965, during the time of the council. Furthermore, the seeds of see-judge-act bore fruit in the *communidades eclesiales de base* and liberation theology movements of South and Central America—that served as irritants to more institutionally-minded members of the Catholic hierarchy, including the young Jesuit provincial Jorge Borgoglio.

Gospel Actualized Community

One of the first pastoral concerns expressed by the bishops at Vatican II—in *Sacrosanctum Concilium* (The Constitution on the Sacred Liturgy)—was that through preaching the church avail itself more abundantly of the riches of Sacred Scripture. They said, "The ministry of preaching should be carried out properly and with the greatest of care. The primary source of the sermon, moreover, should be scripture and liturgy, for in them is found the proclamation of God's wonderful works in the history of salvation, the mystery of Christ ever made present and active within us, especially in the celebration of the liturgy" (35).[4] The bishops also said:

> The treasures of the bible are to be opened up more lavishly, so that a richer fare may be provided for the faithful at the table of God's word. In this way the more signifi-

cant part of the sacred scriptures will be read to the people
over a fixed number of years.

By means of the homily, the mysteries of the faith and
the guiding principles of the christian life are expounded
from the sacred text during the course of the liturgical
year. The homily is strongly recommended since it forms
part of the liturgy itself. In fact, at those Masses which are
celebrated on Sundays and holydays of obligation, with
the people assisting, it should not be omitted except for
a serious reason (51–52).[5]

Some thirty years later, the Pontifical Biblical Commission
picked up this theme in a discussion on the use of the Bible in
the liturgy:

> From the earliest days of the church, the reading of Scrip-
> ture has been an integral part of the Christian liturgy, an
> inheritance to some extent from the liturgy of the syna-
> gogue. Today, too, it is above all through the liturgy that
> Christians come into contact with Scripture, particularly
> during the Sunday celebration of the Eucharist.
>
> In principle, the liturgy, and especially the sacramental
> liturgy, the high point of which is the eucharistic celebra-
> tion, brings about the most perfect actualization of the
> biblical texts, for the liturgy places the proclamation in
> the midst of the community of believers, gathered around
> Christ so as to draw near to God. Christ is then "present
> in his word, because it is he himself who speaks when
> sacred Scripture is read in the church." Written text thus
> becomes living word.
>
> The liturgical reform initiated by the Second Vatican
> Council sought to provide Catholics with rich sustenance
> from the Bible.[6]

Any consideration of theological reflection invites ongoing
consideration as to how the word of God in Holy Scripture
animates today's believing community. Vatican II placed the
homily at the forefront of a Catholic appropriation of the Scriptures. From the perspective of experience, however, it seems
increasingly evident that the brief span of the Sunday homily

cannot sustain the entire burden of the ministry of the Word for a Christian community. As composer Leonard Bernstein's *Mass* said in 1971, "You cannot imprison the Word of the Lord." Certainly, we cannot imprison God's Word to the brief eight to ten minutes of a Sunday preaching and think we are doing justice to the enormity of what God has said and can say to the church through the lens of the Scriptures.

One of the most often quoted and remembered statements of Vatican II is the sentence in the *Constitution on the Sacred Liturgy* that famously said in 1963 that "the liturgy is the summit [*culmen*] toward which the activity of the Church is directed; it is also the source [*fons*] from which all its flows" (10). Given that the eucharistic liturgy is understood to be a dual action with Liturgy of the Word and Liturgy of the Eucharist, the Liturgy of the Word can then be understood as "the summit toward which the activity of the church's ministry of the Word is directed and also the font or source from which all the Word's power flows." While *culmen et fons* commonly has been referenced with the phrase *summit and source*, clearly a more precise rendering is *summit and font*—a reference that closely aligns the eucharistic table with the baptismal font. How, accordingly, is the church's ministry of the Word to be understood, both as summit and font, and also in terms of full baptismal participation?

Following the communal and participative instincts of Vatican II, the eucharistic homily can be understood as summit and source in relation to a ministry of the Word that pervades every aspect of the community of faith. *Fulfilled in Your Hearing* gives a great clue to the scope of the ministry of the Word in what can be called a Gospel Actualized Community by saying that the Sunday homily "may well include evangelization, catechesis, and exhortation" (42).[7] This is to say, then, that the homily is summit and source of a ministry of the Word expressed communally in evangelization, catechesis, and exhortation. These three ministries of the Word align with the three worlds of experience that the Whiteheads say are brought into conversation in theological reflection: "the community of faith, the Christian tradition, and the resources of the culture."

In a fascinating way, this entire schema is holographic or fractal—with each communal arena of the ministry of the Word making present the entire community and the entire church in microcosm. In whatever dimension of the Gospel Actualized Community the ministry of the Word is practiced, the dialogue partners are church—whole and complete. For example, in the Rite of Christian Initiation, the ministry of the Word that we call catechesis is a theological reflection that brings the religiously relevant worlds of experience of individual believers, the Christian tradition, and institutional and cultural factors into conversation and dialogue. The Rite of Christian Initiation also finds its summit and font in the word and sacrament of the ecclesial rites of initiation. In the catechumenate, as in other expressions of authentic catechesis, the experience of church is whole and complete. And, as Pope John Paul II made clear in his apostolic exhortation *Catechesi Tradendae* (On Catechesis in Our Time), catechesis is integral to the evangelization of which all recent popes speak: "*Evangelii nuntiandi* . . . rightly stressed that evangelization—that has the aim of bringing the Good News to the whole of humanity, so that all may live by it—is a rich, complex, and dynamic reality, made up of elements, or one could say moments, that are essential and different from each other, and that must all be kept in view simultaneously. Catechesis is one of these moments . . . in the whole process of evangelization" (18).[8]

Later in the document, John Paul further spells out this relation between catechesis and evangelization of culture:

> The term "acculturation" or "inculturation" may be a neologism, but it expresses very well one factor of the great mystery of the Incarnation. We can say of catechesis, as well as of evangelization in general, that it is called to bring the power of the Gospel into the very heart of culture and cultures. For this purpose, catechesis will seek to know these cultures and their essential components; it will learn their most significant expressions; it will respect their particular values and riches. In this manner it will be able to offer these cultures the knowledge of the

hidden mystery and help them to bring forth from their
own living tradition original expressions of Christian life,
celebration and thought. (53)

Pope Paul also observed that catechesis finds its summit and
source in the homily, and that the church's catechetical project
requires good and frequent preaching:

> the homily takes up again the journey of faith put forward
> by catechesis, and brings it to its natural fulfillment. . . .
> Accordingly, one can say that catechetical teaching too
> finds its source and its fulfillment in the Eucharist, within
> the whole circle of the liturgical year. Preaching, centered
> upon the Bible texts, must then in its own way make it
> possible to familiarize the faithful with the whole of the
> mysteries of the faith and with the norms of Christian
> living. Much attention must be given to the homily: it
> should be neither too long nor too short; it should always
> be carefully prepared, rich in substance and adapted to the
> hearers, and reserved to ordained ministers. The homily
> should have its place not only in every Sunday and feast-
> day Eucharist, but also in the celebration of baptisms,
> penitential liturgies, marriages and funerals. This is one
> of the benefits of the liturgical renewal. (48)

The fractal composition of the church's ministry of the
Word likewise is present in the many forms of exhortation
that support individuals in the community of faith: pastoral
care, spiritual companionship, friendship, and testimony. Each
of these expressions of the Word engage individuals in a dialogue with the church's cumulative experience of communities
of living faith, the vast resources of the church's faith tradition
(Scripture, sacrament, doctrine, and spirituality), and life as
experienced through culture, institutions, and systems. Each of
these modes of exhortation and mutual support likewise find
expression in a liturgical or sacramental summit and source—
for example, in the sacraments of reconciliation, anointing of
the sick, and marriage. This fractal quality of spiritual exhortation and companionship is so essentially baptismal and invites

appreciative reflection. When we companion one another in faith, we are church—whole and complete.

A consideration of the church's ministry of the Word in dialogues with culture calls to mind two important theological terms: inculturation and evangelization. Whereas the words *enculturation* and *acculturation* are sociological terms for the processes of growing into and taking on one's own culture or another culture, *inculturation* is a theological term for the process of mutual encounter between gospel tradition, as represented by the institutional church and its evangelists, and particular cultures. Inculturation takes place in a three-stage process of *translation, assimilation,* and *transformation.*

The first step is a simple translation of the Scriptures and of other artifacts of the tradition into the languages of the people—a one-directional movement of Gospel to culture. In the second step, the culture assimilates the Gospel, allowing the Gospel to express itself in the cultural metaphors, customs, and practices of the people. This, in turn, can lead to a third step of more critical assimilation in which the encounter with the Gospel transforms culture to be more aligned as an expression on Earth of the paradigmatic vision of the *basileia* or reign of God.

At this level of cultural encounter with the Gospel, inculturated disciple communities take their place in the emergent tradition of discipleship and in the communion of communities that is the institutional church. In a communitarian vision of the *basileia* of God, the transforming effects of this encounter are mutual. This evangelization of culture, as Pope Paul VI called it, or this new evangelization as Pope John Paul II called it, are meant to be understood in terms of mutual influence and transformation, in marked contrast to the operative understanding of mission in the course of centuries of cultural conquest. Only when church mission to culture is understood in terms of a mutually transformative encounter can we begin to speak, as the church does today, of reverse mission—as in the case of indigenous and marginalized peoples addressing the Good News of much-needed gospel correctives to the dominant cultural practices of their colonizers and of those disciples from other cultures who have reached out to accompany them. Inculturation is a story of civic communities and cultures aligning themselves with Christianity in a way that expresses the whole and complete church.

Pope Francis is no stranger to the joys and sufferings of God's people, to the riches of the Catholic tradition, or to the peripheries of life in the real world. He seems to have engaged people of goodwill throughout the world in conversations about things that matter. The ministry of the Word in all its manifestations, even the liturgical homily, is essentially a constitutive conversation of the church. *Fulfilled in Your Hearing,* in Section IV on Homiletic Style, says of the liturgical homily: "As regards the structure and style of the homily, we can take a lead from the use of the Greek word *homileo* in the New Testament. While the etymology of the word suggests communicating with a crowd, its actual use in the New Testament implies a more personal and conversational form of address than that used by the classical Greek orator. . . . The New Testament usage suggests that a homily should sound more like a personal conversation, albeit a conversation on matters of utmost importance, than like a speech or classroom lecture" (63).

This conversational tone of homiletic preaching is more than a matter of oratory—it pertains also to the pervasive and fractal nature of the communal conversation characteristic of the ministry of the Word throughout the Gospel Actualized Community—a pervasive conversation in the light of faith about things that matter for which the homily, in all its liturgical and sacramental iterations, is summit and source—*culmen et fons*.

Pope Francis's Call to Missionary Discipleship

In his preaching and teaching conversation with people, churches and religions, and civic institutions throughout the world, Pope Francis consistently invites all believers and people of goodwill according to their station in life into *missionary discipleship*. The missionary aspect, of course, has to do with being sent and going out on mission on behalf of the reign of

God—as opposed to the many self-referential sins too often associated with the pursuits of life, spirituality, and society. But what is meant by the discipleship aspect of missionary discipleship? Christian discipleship can be defined as *participative action on behalf of the reign of God in a circle of reflective discourse as the people of God.* Christian community is a web of relationships, of which Catholic theologian Richard R. Gaillardetz writes: "We might say then that the church is both a community or gathering of disciples and at the same time a kind of 'school of discipleship.' We gather in the full expectation that membership in the Christian community will lay claim to the entirety of our existence. Everything in our lives must be assessed and interpreted within the matrix of beliefs and practices that make this community distinctive. We are 'schooled' as disciples when we allow our participation in this community to shed light on every aspect of our existence."[9]

Gaillardetz goes on to list four essential practices of Christian discipleship. *Kerygma* customarily refers to the essential Gospel message to be proclaimed as Good News. *Leitourgia* (liturgy) is a word taking its origins in the responsibility of all citizens to do their share in a public project, such as building a wall or a road, and that can be taken to refer to our participation in the liturgical assembly for the sake of being sent into action on behalf of the reign of God. Full, conscious, and active participation in the liturgy forms and builds authentic Christian community or *koinonia,* and it is the community that calls and sends us to missionary service or *diakonia.* Taken together, these practices give expression to missionary discipleship.

A more detailed meditation on *Christian discipleship as participative action on behalf of the reign of God in a circle of reflective discourse as the people of God* might be mapped out as seen in the diagram on page 30.

In his call to engaged discipleship, Pope Francis invites believers to the deepest sources and purposes of Christian life. As we embrace this life of discipleship in communities of intentionality and purpose, our lives and our world become a crucible of transformation for the reign of God.

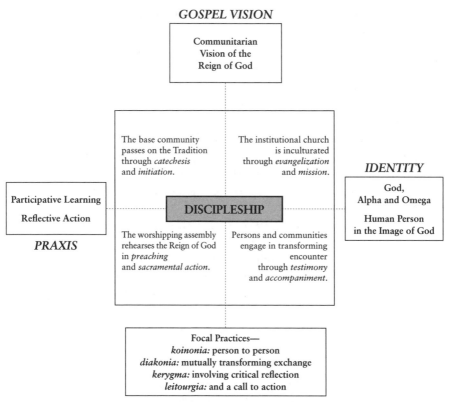

GOSPEL VISION

Communitarian
Vision of the
Reign of God

The base community
passes on the Tradition
through *catechesis*
and *initiation*.

The institutional church
is inculturated
through *evangelization*
and *mission*.

IDENTITY

God,
Alpha and Omega

Human Person
in the Image of God

Participative Learning

Reflective Action

DISCIPLESHIP

PRAXIS

The worshipping assembly
rehearses the Reign of God
in *preaching*
and *sacramental action*.

Persons and communities
engage in transforming
encounter
through *testimony*
and *accompaniment*.

Focal Practices—
koinonia: person to person
diakonia: mutually transforming exchange
kerygma: involving critical reflection
leitourgia: and a call to action

DISCIPLE COMMUNITY

The Church's Transforming Encounter with Society

As Pope Francis issues his signature invitation for all believers
to embrace a vocation of missionary discipleship at the peripheries, those peripheries can be broadly defined to include the
home, the workplace, the many institutions that constitute the
profit and nonprofit sectors of the economy, as well as political
entities from local to regional to national and global. At every
periphery, the church wishes to attend to the human person
and especially to the poor, the oppressed, the marginalized.

Pope Francis's call to discipleship at the peripheries gives
witness to the relevance and sophistication of the body of

Catholic Social Teaching that the church and successive papacies have been spelling out since Pius XI's encyclical letter *Rerum Novarum* (On Human Labor) in 1891. In this body of literature, the following principles have merged as a cumulative framework for Catholic social ethics:

- Every human being is a person, with inalienable rights and corresponding duties.
- Human beings are interdependent.
- The human person is the foundation and end of all human institutions.
- The family is the most autonomous and fundamental human institution.
- State authority properly flows from moral force and rule of law.
- Intermediate institutions between family and state also serve the common good.
- Human institutions are interrelated according to a principle of subsidiarity.
- The church respects the legitimate autonomy of the democratic order.

- Work is a constitutive dimension of human life.
- The proper subject of work is the human person, not capital.
- Workers have rights to private property, just wages, and to labor unions.
- The common good includes just distribution of the world's goods.
- An economic system should allow free work, enterprise, and participation.

- Peace is built on a foundation of justice.
- Development is the path to peace.

- The social structures of sin are radically opposed to peace and development.

- Solidarity is the moral response to interdependence and social sin.

————

- The church has made a fundamental option on behalf of the poor.

- Social doctrine is a constitutive aspect of the Gospel and of evangelization.

Without question, Pope Francis understands his ministry and his message to the world from within this Catholic Social Teaching context. Pope Paul VI's encyclical letter *Evangelii Nuntiandi* (On Evangelization in the Modern World) also is important because it draws a direct link from Catholic Social Teaching to the idea of evangelization:

> The Gospel, and therefore evangelization, are certainly not identical with culture, and they are independent in regard to all cultures. . . . Though independent of cultures, the Gospel and evangelization are not necessarily incompatible with them; rather they are capable of permeating them all without becoming subject to any one of them.
>
> The split between the Gospel and the culture is without a doubt the drama of our time, just as it was of other times. Therefore every effort must be made to ensure a full evangelization of culture, or more correctly of cultures. They have to be regenerated by an encounter with the Gospel. But this encounter will not take place if the Gospel is not proclaimed. (20)[10]

Paul VI wrote that "evangelization involves an explicit message, adapted to the different situations constantly being realized, about the rights and duties of every human being, about family life without which personal growth and development is hardly possible, about life in society, about international life, peace, justice, and development—a message especially energetic today about liberation" (29). Evangelization, therefore in large measure, is an apostolic work of the laity:

> Lay people, whose particular vocation places them in the midst of the world and in charge of the most varied temporal tasks, must for this very reason exercise a very special form of evangelization.
>
> Their primary and immediate task is not to establish and develop the ecclesial community—this is the specific role of the pastors—but to put to use every Christian and evangelical possibility latent but already present and active in the affairs of the world. Their own field of evangelizing activity is the vast and complicated world of politics, society and economics, but also the world of culture, of the sciences and the arts, of international life, of the mass media. It also includes other realities which are open to evangelization, such as human love, the family, the education of children and adolescents, professional work, suffering. (70)

As Pope Francis invites us by virtue of baptism and according to our station in life to be missionary disciples and evangelists, we are given a great opportunity—to put on the cloak of Catholic Social Teaching, to take up the Word of the Lord, and to go to the peripheries on behalf of the reign of God.

3
The Gospel Preached with Unction

A good priest can be recognized by the way his people are anointed: this is a clear proof. When our people are anointed with the oil of gladness, it is obvious: for example, when they leave Mass looking as if they have heard good news. Our people like to hear the Gospel preached with "unction," they like it when the Gospel we preach touches their daily lives, when it runs down like the oil of Aaron to the edges of reality, when it brings light to moments of extreme darkness, to the "outskirts" where people of faith are most exposed to the onslaught of those who want to tear down their faith. People thank us because they feel that we have prayed over the realities of their everyday lives, their troubles, their joys, their burdens and their hopes. . . .

We need to "go out," then, in order to experience our own anointing, its power and its redemptive efficacy: to the "outskirts" where there is suffering, bloodshed, blindness that longs for sight, and prisoners in thrall to many evil masters. It is not in soul-searching or constant introspection that we encounter the Lord: self-help courses can be useful in life, but to live our priestly life going from one course to another, from one method to another, leads us to become Pelagians and to minimize the power of grace, which comes alive and flourishes to the extent that we, in faith, go out and give ourselves and the Gospel to others,

giving what little ointment we have to those who have
nothing, nothing at all.

—Pope Francis, Homily at the Chrism Mass
Vatican Basilica, March 28, 2013[1]

Fulfilled in Your Hearing

Fulfilled in Your Hearing: the Homily in the Sunday Assembly,
issued in 1982 by the Bishops' Committee on Priestly Life and
Ministry of the United States Catholic Conference (now the
United States Conference of Catholic Bishops), was written
over the space of two years in a highly consultative process.
While a committee of twelve bishops, priests, and scholars undertook this task with many others, the principal writers were
William Skudlarek, OSB, from St. John's Abbey in Minnesota,
and Fred Baumer, CPPS, from Chicago.[2]

The document's introductory section begins with an important assertion: "The primary duty of priests is the proclamation
of the Gospel of God to all," and, "The other duties of the priest
are to be considered properly presbyteral to the degree that they
support the proclamation of the Gospel." Similar assertions
also are made of the importance of preaching in the ministry
of deacons and of the statement that "the proclamation of the
Word of God is the responsibility of the entire Christian community by virtue of the sacrament of baptism"—especially in
the case of the catechumenate. This emphasis, of course, is not
original to the bishops in the United States; rather, they are
echoing the pastoral insights of the Second Vatican Council, as
put forth in the *Decree on the Ministry and Life of Priests* in
1965: "The People of God is formed into in the first place by
the word of the living God, which is quite rightly expected from
the mouth of priests. For since nobody can be saved who has
not first believed, it is the first task of priests as co-workers of
the bishops to preach the Gospel of God to all. In this way they
carry out the Lord's command 'Go into all the world and preach
the Gospel to every creature' (Mk 16:15), and thus establish

and increase the people of God. For by the saving word of God faith is aroused in the heart of unbelievers and is nourished in the heart of believers. By this faith then the congregation of the faithful begins and grows, according to the saying of the apostle: 'Faith comes from what is heard, and what is heard comes by the preaching of Christ' (Rom 10:17)" (4).[3]

Fulfilled in Your Hearing has proven both early on and over time to be a classic contribution to the literature of pastoral and theological implementation of Vatican II. And as with most ecclesiastical classics, its compositional structure itself communicates the insight and message in a significant way. The main corpus of the document is laid out very simply in a sequence of three sections: first the Assembly, then the Preacher, then the Homily.

As this document considers the meaning of liturgical preaching, the listening assembly holds privilege of place. Only by first considering the role and needs of the discipleship assembly, can we understand the ministerial role and responsibilities of the preacher with clarity. *Fulfilled in Your Hearing* calls the preacher a mediator of meaning to the liturgical assembly: "The person who preaches in the context of the liturgical assembly is thus a mediator, representing both the community and the Lord" (12). "The preacher acts as a mediator; making connections between the real lives of people . . . and the God who calls us into ever deeper communion with himself and with one another. Especially in the Eucharistic celebration, . . . the preacher is called to point to the signs of God's presence in the lives of his people." (15).[4]

Preachers are tasked to interpret the lives and contexts of the worshipping faithful through the Scriptures, the liturgy, the signs of the times, and church teaching: "The homily is not so much *on* the Scriptures as *from* and *through* them" (50) and "the preacher does not so much attempt to explain the Scriptures as to interpret the human situation through the Scriptures. In other words, the goal of the liturgical preacher is not to interpret a text of the Bible (as would be the case in teaching a Scripture class) as much as to draw on the texts of the Bible as they are presented in the lectionary to interpret peoples' lives" (52). Only when preaching is properly understood in this way as a pastorally hermeneutical act, does *Fulfilled in Your Hearing* in chapter 3 give consideration to the homily—the rhetorical expression of this interpretive mediation of meaning between preacher and assembly.

Tellingly, *Fulfilled in Your Hearing* explores the etymological roots of the Greek word *homileo* in reference to the scriptural conversation by the risen Lord with the disciples on the road to Emmaus: "New Testament usage suggests that a homily should sound more like a personal conversation, albeit conversation on matters of most importance, than like a speech or a classroom lecture. What we should strive for is a style that is purposeful and personal, avoiding whatever sounds casual and chatty . . . or impersonal and detached" (63).[5] Good preaching is less about classical oratory and more about the pastoral conversation by the preacher with the assembly—a conversation among disciples that mediates meaning.

In the preaching of his first chrism Mass as cited earlier in the first chapter, Pope Francis went on to say, "When we have this relationship with God and with his people, and grace passes through us, then we are priests, mediators between God and men."[6] This is not a cultic mediation. For Pope Francis, it is a heart-to-heart communication in which the faithful, both preacher and listeners, go out to the peripheries and outskirts of real life with all its joy, suffering, and hope. And this interpretative mediation of reality through the eyes and ears of faith, as we will see in *Evangelii Gaudium*, is a core and constitutive practice of the faith and a responsibility of all the faithful, both preacher and listener alike. We all are being called and sent by Pope Francis to the ordinary places and to the peripheries of life to be evangelists and missionary disciples.

Whether or not Pope Francis has himself studied *Fulfilled in Your Hearing*—an American document—he proves himself consistently to be aligned with its priorities and insights as found in the pastoral teaching of Vatican II. And he also has given us an interpretive tool for critiquing preaching, preachers, and listening assemblies in light of these pastoral priorities and insights. As mentioned earlier, when speaking in his brief pre-conclave address to the cardinal electors, Archbishop Borgoglio critiqued the church as too "self-referential" and even as "sick." Homilies, preachers, and assemblies can fall into self-referential bad habits—sometimes distressingly to the point of being sick. A homily, for example, can focus self-referentially on exegesis of a text—to the exclusion of mediating meaning in a pastoral dialogue with the joys, sufferings, and hopes of the listening faithful. Or a homily can focus so self-referentially on a church teaching or doctrine—again without pastoral reference to the complexity of the people's lived experience—as to be preachy or even a diatribe.

Preachers also are widely experienced to be self-referential—talking about themselves to the exclusion of the text. These preachings can be boring and infuriating or they can be interesting and entertaining, but they do not interpret the lives of the listeners by means of a pastoral conversation with the scriptural texts, the liturgy, or church tradition. Properly speaking, these self-referential preachings are not homilies. A preaching may sound good but at the worst can be inherently self-absorbed—lacking authenticity at the core.

Listening assemblies, too, can lack gospel authenticity by virtue of being too self-referential—taking a consumer mentality in respect to the church and liturgy, expressing self-satisfaction to the point of stunting a congregation's embrace or expression of the faith or of missionary discipleship, excluding outsiders or even congregational insiders from participation, or demeaning and resisting the good intentions of clergy, lay ministers, or ministerial volunteers.

Pope Francis, both in his message and in the authenticity of his person, invites us beyond these sins. If he were writing *Fulfilled in Your Hearing*, perhaps he would insert a preliminary chapter before the assembly, before the preacher, before the homily—giving priority to all the real-world peripheries from which we are called and to which we are sent to be faith-filled missionary disciples of Jesus Christ alive and active in our midst.

The Homily as Summit and Source

In 2013 Pope Francis made what may prove to be the most significant magisterial contribution to the Roman Catholic homiletic literature since the American bishops issued *Fulfilled in Your Hearing* in 1982. In November 2013 on the Solemnity of Our Lord Jesus Christ, King of the Universe, Francis issued his apostolic exhortation *Evangelii Gaudium* (The Joy of the Gospel).[7]

In chapter 3 of this lengthy five-chapter document, the pope inserted two sections on "The homily" and on "Preparing to preach" at the very center of this four-section middle chapter and of the five-chapter document—at the midpoint of the mid-chapter of the hanging chain of ideas of the entire text. In this chapter, the two centermost sections on the homily and on preparing to preach are preceded by a first section on the universal call to all baptized believers to be missionary disciples and evangelists—"The entire people of God proclaims the Gospel"—and a concluding fourth section on the call to some of the faithful to serve as catechists and teachers—"Evangelization and the deeper understanding of the kerygma." In chapter 3, therefore, the homily takes on a central place of service to the pope's discussion of evangelization and to the church's entire ministry of the Word.

In his opening paragraphs on the homily, Pope Francis says, "The homily is the touchstone for judging the pastor's closeness and ability to communicate to his people. We know that the faithful attach great importance to it, and that both they and their ordained ministers suffer because of homilies" (135). He then addresses "the liturgical context of homiletic preaching," saying that the homily "surpasses all forms of catechesis as the supreme moment in the dialogue between God and his people which lead up to sacramental communion" (137) and "The homily cannot be a form of entertainment like those presented by the media, yet it does need to give life and meaning to the celebration. It is a distinctive genre; . . . it should be brief and avoid taking on any semblance of a speech or a lecture" (138).

It seems that one of Pope Francis's favorite images for the ministry is that of the minister as a sweet and comforting mother. Here, he describes preaching as "a mother's conversation" and says that "a good mother can recognize everything that God is bringing about in her children, she listens to their concerns and learns from them. . . . Something similar happens in a homily" (139).

Pope Francis says that preaching uses "words which set hearts on fire," and in words reminiscent of Cicero's and Augustine's "to teach, to delight, and to persuade," Pope Francis writes: "Dialogue is much more than the communication of a truth. It arises from the enjoyment of speaking and it enriches those who express their love for one another through the medium of words. This is an enrichment which does not consist in objects but in persons who share themselves in dialogue. A preaching which would be purely moralistic or doctrinaire or one which turns into a lecture on biblical exegesis detracts from this heart-to-heart communication which takes place in the homily and possesses a quasi-sacramental character" (142).

This caution by Pope Francis about moralistic or doctrinaire preaching comes less than a year after the United States Conference of Catholic Bishops issued their document on *Preaching the Mystery of Faith,* that addressed considerable concern to the doctrinal and catechetical purposes of preaching. The American bishops wrote:

> Certainly, doctrine is not meant to be propounded in a homily in the way that it might unfold in a theology classroom or a lecture for an academic audience or even a catechism lesson. The homily is integral to the liturgical act of the Eucharist, and the language and spirit of the homily should fit that context. Yet catechesis in its broadest sense involves the effective communication of the full scope of the Church's teaching and formation, from initiation into the Sacrament of Baptism through the moral requirements of a faithful Christian life. The *Catechism* itself is organized into four "pillars" of Christian life, reflecting on the Creed, the celebration of the Christian mystery in our liturgical and sacramental life, the moral responsibilities of life in Christ, and finally, the meaning of Christian prayer. Over time the homilist,

> while respecting the unique form and spirit of the Sunday homily, should communicate the full scope of this rich catechetical teaching to his congregation. During the course of the liturgical year it is appropriate to offer the faithful, prudently and on the basis of the three-year Lectionary, "'thematic' homilies treating the great themes of the Christian faith."
>
> Making a thoughtful and integral connection between the Scripture passages proclaimed in the Eucharist and the requirements of Christian belief and life should also be keyed to the seasons of the liturgical year: reflection on the ultimate purpose and direction of our lives in the Advent season; the gift of life and the joy of the Incarnation at the Christmas season; the need for repentance and renewal during Lent; the dynamic gift of the Spirit in our lives at Pentecost. (23–24)[8]

Without taking exception to doctrinal or catechetical considerations in preaching, *Evangelii Gaudium*—written in the same year—puts its accent on evangelization and heart-to-heart communication of the Gospel. In his treatment of the homily in chapter 3, he writes: "The challenge of inculturated preaching consists in proclaiming a synthesis, not ideas or detached values. Where your synthesis is, there lies your heart. . . . The word is essentially a mediator and requires not just the two who dialogue but also an intermediary who presents it for what it is, out of the conviction that 'what we preach is not ourselves, but Jesus Christ as Lord, with ourselves as your servants for Jesus' sake' (*2 Cor* 4:5)" (143). These meditations on the homily in 135 to 144 of *Evangelii Gaudium* are entirely consonant with the themes of Pope Francis's preaching and deserve to be looked up and read closely.

Perhaps the best test of the pope's insights in these tightly written paragraphs on the homily is his own preaching. Listening to Pope Francis as he preaches nearly every day and in so many liturgical contexts, our preaching pope models what it means for the preacher to hold a mother's conversation that sets hearts on fire. Everywhere, people remark how Pope Francis in his preaching inspires them to want to be better men, women, and youth. Given that the words of his preaching are not often long remembered, we realize that he in essence communicates the authenticity of his character—making the Good News of Jesus Christ incarnate in his person and in his ministry.

In his 2010 post-synodal exhortation *Verbum Domini*, Pope Benedict XVI spoke at length about the Word of God in the liturgy, the sacramentality of the Word, and the importance of the homily. He also made the following insightful and learned observation about the performative character of the word: "The relationship between word and sacramental gesture is the liturgical expression of God's activity in the history of salvation through the *performative character* of the word itself. In salvation history there is no separation between what God *says* and what he *does*. His word appears as alive and active (cf. Heb 4:12), as the Hebrew term *dabar* itself makes clear. In the liturgical action too, we encounter his word which accomplishes what it says. By educating the People of God to discover the performative character of God's word in the liturgy, we will help them to recognize his activity in salvation history and in their individual lives" (58).[9] This is what Pope Francis is doing: he is performing the Word, and he is teaching us to do the same with our lives.

Preaching as Practice in Holiness

Fulfilled in Your Hearing—after its three significant and memorable chapters on the assembly, the preacher, and the homily—included a fourth, less memorable chapter on homiletic method that outlines preaching's preparation as a process of reading, listening, and praying; study and further reflection; letting go; drafting; revising; practicing; and preaching. The chapter also gives a seven-step process for hosting a homily preparation group.

Pope Francis's thoughts on preparing to preach, also at the lowest center-point of textual service in chapter 3 of *The Joy of the Gospel,* are true to his person—pragmatic, challenging, and deeply spiritual. He starts by saying: "Preparation for preaching is so important a task that a prolonged time of study, prayer, reflection and pastoral creativity should be devoted to it. With great affection I wish to stop for a moment and offer a method of preparing homilies. . . . Some pastors argue that such preparation is not possible given the vast number of tasks which they must perform; nonetheless, I presume to ask that each week a sufficient portion of personal and community time be dedicated to this task, even if less time has to be given to other important activities. . . . A preacher who does not prepare is not spiritual; he is dishonest and irresponsible with the gifts he has received" (145).

Preparation for preaching requires giving one's "entire attention to the biblical text . . . practicing 'reverence for the truth.' This is the humility of heart which recognizes that the Word is always beyond us, that 'we are neither its masters or owners, but its guardians, heralds and servants'" (146, citing Pope Paul VI in *Evangelii Nuntiandi*). Our aim as preachers "is not to understand every little detail of the text; our most important goal is to discover its principal message, the message which gives structure and unity to the text" (147). "One of the defects of a tedious and ineffectual preaching is precisely its inability to transmit the intrinsic power of the text which has been proclaimed" (148).

Pope Francis invites preachers into the work of personalizing the Word: "It is good for us to renew our fervor each day and every Sunday as we prepare the homily, examining ourselves to see if we have grown in love for the word which we preach. Nor should we forget that 'the greater or lesser degree of the holiness of the minister has a real effect on the proclamation of the word'" (149, citing Pope John Paul II in *Pastores Dabo Vobis*).

With an additional citation of Paul VI from *Evangelii Nuntiandi,* Pope Francis appeals to an authentic heart-to-heart testimony on the part of preachers: "People prefer to listen to witnesses: they 'thirst for authenticity' and 'call for evangelizers to speak of a God whom they themselves know and are familiar with, as if they were seeing him'" (150). And citing St. Thomas

Aquinas, Pope Francis asserts: "Whoever wants to preach must be the first to let the word of God move him deeply and become incarnate in his daily life. In this way preaching will consist in that activity, so intense and fruitful, which is 'communicating to others what one has contemplated'" (150, citing *Summa Theologica* II-II, q. 188, a. 6).

In a section on "spiritual reading" in which Pope Francis commends the preacher to the practice of *lectio divina* (152), the Pope invites the preacher to an "encounter with God's word" that avoids the "the common temptation . . . to think about what the text means for other people, and so avoid applying it to our own life" (153). The pope also understands that the preacher must also turn "an ear to the people"; he says: "A preacher has to contemplate the word, but he also has to contemplate his people. . . . Preparation for preaching thus becomes an exercise in evangelical discernment" (154). "We should never respond to questions nobody asks" (155).

In a concluding section on homiletic resources, the pope also speaks briefly about the rhetoric of preaching. Our pope, who is a master of the sermonic image, beautifully reflects: "One of the most important things is to learn how to use images and preaching, how to appeal to imagery. Sometimes examples are used to clarify a certain point, but these examples usually appeal only to the mind; images, on the other hand, help people better to appreciate and accept the message we wish to communicate. An attractive image makes the message seem familiar, close to home, practical and related to everyday life. A successful image can make people [savor] the message, awaken a desire and move the will towards the Gospel. A good homily, an old teacher once told me, should have 'an idea, a sentiment, an image'" (157).

Pope Francis concludes his remarks on preparing to preach by saying, "Another feature of a good homily is that it is positive. It is not so much concerned with pointing out what shouldn't be done, but with suggesting what we can do better. . . . Positive preaching always offers hope, points to the future, does not leave us trapped in negativity" (159).

This third section, on preparing to preach, in chapter 3 of *The Joy of the Gospel* succeeds beautifully in giving helpful rhetorical tips on preparing to preach, and these meditations might most properly be read as a spirituality of preaching. As *Fulfilled in Your Hearing* acknowledges—given the diverse contexts of preaching and the varied personalities and styles of individual preachers—there is no one way to prepare to preach. In every context and for every preacher, however, preaching is a contemplative act that calls upon a spirituality of heart-to-heart communication—with God, with the scriptural and liturgical text, and, of course, with the people and the signs of the times.

4
We Testify to the Word with Our Lives

> My mission of being in the heart of the people is not just part of my life or a badge I can take off; it is not an "extra" or just another moment in life. Instead, it is something I cannot uproot from my being without destroying my very self. I have a mission on this earth; that is the reason why I am here in this world. We have to regard ourselves as sealed, even branded, by this mission of bringing light, blessing, enlivening, raising up, healing and freeing. All around us we begin to see nurses with soul, teachers with soul, politicians with soul, people who have chosen deep down to be with others and for others. (273)
>
> —Pope Francis on "Spirit Filled Evangelizers,"
> Chapter Five, *The Joy of the Gospel*[1]

Missionary Disciples and Evangelists

If one were to list magisterial documents that most clearly spell out a Roman Catholic vision of preaching since the Second Vatican Council, that list could well include the Constitution on the Sacred Liturgy (*Sacrosanctum Concilium*, 1963); On Evangelization in the Modern World (*Evangelii Nuntiandi*), promulgated by Pope Paul VI on the tenth anniversary of the closing of Vatican II (1975); the Pontifical Biblical Commission on *The Interpretation of the Bible in the Church* (1994);

Pope Benedict XVI's apostolic exhortation *Verbum Domini* (2010); and—in the United States—*Fulfilled in Your Hearing: the Homily in the Sunday Assembly* (1982) and *Preaching the Mystery of Faith* (2013).

It might surprise most people, however, to also include the 1983 *Code of Canon Law*.[2] Doing so, many preachers might reflexively turn to canon 767.1, that says, "Among the forms of preaching, the homily, which is part of the liturgy itself and is reserved to a priest or deacon, is preeminent; in the homily the mysteries of faith and the norms of Christian life are to be explained from the sacred text during the course of the liturgical year."

Ecclesiastical authorities certainly have labored to put to rest the troublesome question of who may preach the liturgical homily.[3] Very little attention, however, has been given to canon 211, that simply reads: "All the Christian faithful have the duty and right to work so that the divine message of salvation more and more reaches all people in every age and in every land." Like a grain of sand that over time produces a pearl of great price, this hidden sentence—something so new in all of canon law—presaged something altogether fresh and precious in the self-understanding of the church—that we, all of us, are missionary disciples and evangelists.[4] This is the pearl of great price in *Evangelii Gaudium*.

Like our pope, and like his namesake St. Francis, we all are called by virtue of our Christian baptism to take the faith into our world, testifying to what we have heard and seen and touched in Christ. Liturgical preaching—discussed at the very center of Pope Francis's apostolic exhortation *Evangelii Gaudium*—is best understood as the "summit and font" of this universal testimony and accompaniment as missionary disciples and evangelists. This universal testimony and accompaniment is the very point of the apostolic exhortation that Pope Francis on the title page of the document addresses "to the bishops, clergy, consecrated persons, and the lay faithful on the proclamation of the Gospel in today's world."

Pope Francis makes this point assertively in the opening section of chapter 3 of *The Joy of the Gospel*. The church and the people of God are on a mission:

> The church, as the agent of evangelization, is more than an organic and hierarchical institution; . . . she exists concretely in history as a people of pilgrims and evangelizers, transcending any institutional expression, however necessary. (111)

> Jesus did not tell the apostles to form an exclusive and elite group. He said: "Go and make disciples of all nations" (Mt 28:19). (113)

> In all the baptized, from first to last, the sanctifying power of the Spirit is it work, impelling us to evangelization. . . . God furnishes the totality of the faithful with an instinct of faith—*sensus fidei*—which helps them to discern what is truly of God. (119)

> All the baptized, whatever their position in the church or their level of instruction in the faith, are agents of evangelization, and it would be insufficient to envision the plan of the evangelization to be carried out by professionals while the rest of the faithful would simply be passive recipients: . . . we no longer say that we are "disciples" and "missionaries," but rather that we are always "missionary disciples." (120)

> There is a kind of preaching which falls to each of us as a daily responsibility . . . a testimony. (127)

The pope then further brackets his reflection on homiletic preaching in the second and third sections of chapter 3 with a closing fourth section on the need of missionary disciples for formational catechesis. He writes:

> Evangelization aims at a process of growth which entails taking seriously each person and God's plan for his or her life. All of us need to grow in Christ. Evangelization should stimulate a desire for this growth, so that each of us can say wholeheartedly: "It is no longer I who live, but Christ lives in me" (Gal 2:20). It would not be right to

see this call to growth exclusively or primarily in terms of doctrinal formation. . . . Education and catechesis are at the service of this growth. (160–163)

The centrality of the kerygma calls for stressing those elements which are most needed today: it has to express God's saving love which precedes any moral and religious obligation on our part; it should not impose the truth but appeal to freedom; it should be marked by joy, encouragement, liveliness and a harmonious balance. (165)

In *The Joy of the Gospel,* the pope's discussion of homiletical preaching is nestled within a clarion call to all believers to be sent forth (from the liturgy as summit and font of the church's ministry of the Word) on mission—as missionary disciples and evangelists. This—more than anything—is Pope Francis's message in both his preaching and his teaching: we all, according to our baptismal station in life, are preachers of the Good News of Jesus Christ.

The Church's Missionary Transformation

Chapter 3 of *The Joy of the Gospel*—on "The Proclamation of the Gospel"—is the living center of Pope Francis's apostolic exhortation to all the faithful. This lively discussion is supported in the first two chapters by Pope Francis's discussion of "The Church's Missionary Transformation" (chapter 1) and "The Crisis of Communal Commitment" (chapter 2).

As with chapter 3, chapter 1 includes five sections, of which the middle or third section—"From the heart of the Gospel"—may be read to be at the heart of the missionary transformation that Pope Francis sees the church to be experiencing, and that may also be read as Pope Francis's answer to a question that he is putting to the church. He is challenging the church "to put all things in a missionary key." In this center section, he begins by saying: "If we attempt to put all things in a missionary key, this will also affect the way we communicate the message" (34). He writes: "Pastoral ministry in the missionary style is not obsessed with the disjointed transmission of a multitude of doctrines to be insistently imposed. When we adopt a pastoral goal and a missionary style which would actually reach everyone without exception or exclusion, the message has to concentrate on the essentials, on what is most beautiful, most grand, most appealing and at the same time most necessary" (35).

Noting a hierarchy of virtues in Thomas Aquinas's moral teaching, Pope Francis says, "What counts above all else is 'faith working through love' (Gal 5:6); . . . mercy is the greatest of all virtues" (37). "In preaching the Gospel a fitting sense of proportion has to be maintained" (38). The Pope cautions against speaking "more about law than about grace, more about the Church than about Christ, more about the Pope than about God's word" (38).

> Christian morality is not a form of stoicism, or self-denial, or merely a practical philosophy or a catalogue of sins and faults. Before all else, the Gospel invites us to respond to the God of love who saves us, to seek God in others and to go forth from ourselves to seek the good of others. Under no circumstance can this invitation be obscured! All of the virtues are at the service of this response of love. If this invitation does not radiate forcefully and attractively, the edifice of the Church's moral teaching risks becoming a house of cards, and this is our greatest risk. It would mean that it is not the gospel which is being preached, but certain doctrinal or moral points based on specific theological options. The message will run the risk of losing its freshness and will cease to have "the fragrance of the Gospel." (39)

This fragrant, loving Gospel is the Good News we preach as missionary disciples and evangelists. Pope Francis opens chapter 1, saying, "Evangelization takes place in obedience to the missionary mandate of Jesus" (19), and he goes on to say: "An evangelizing community gets involved by word and deed in people's daily lives; it bridges distances, it is willing to abase itself if necessary, and it embraces human life, touching the suffering flesh of Christ in others. Evangelists must take on the 'smell of the sheep' and the sheep are willing to hear their voice" (24).

This sending forth on evangelizing mission both feeds into the celebration of the church's liturgy and finds its vocational commission in it. As Pope Francis puts it in his concluding sentence to the first section on "A church which goes forth" in this first chapter on "The Church's Missionary Transformation," "The Church evangelizes and is herself evangelized through the beauty of the liturgy, which is both a celebration of the task of evangelization and the source of her renewed self-giving" (24).

In chapter 1's second section on "Pastoral activity and conversion," Pope Francis confesses: "I dream of a 'missionary option,' that is, a missionary impulse capable of transforming everything, so that the Church's customs, ways of doing things, times and schedules, language and structures can be suitably channeled for the evangelization of today's world rather than for her self-preservation. . . . All renewal in the Church must have mission as its goal if it is not to fall prey to a kind of ecclesiastical introversion" (27).

A New Evangelization

As Pope Paul VI wrote to all the faithful in his 1975 apostolic exhortation *On Evangelization in the Modern World*, the Second Vatican Council had one objective: "to make the Church of the twentieth century ever better fitted for proclaiming the Gospel to the people of the twentieth century" (2).[5] Pope Paul also gave a social-gospel valence and a Catholic understanding to the word *evangelization*, and coined the expression *evangelization of culture*: "Though independent of cultures, the Gospel and evangelization are not necessarily incompatible with them; rather they are capable of permeating them all without becoming subject to any of them. The split between the Gospel and culture is without a doubt the drama of our time, just as it was of other times. Therefore every effort must be made to ensure a full evangelization of culture, or more correctly of cultures. They have to be regenerated by an encounter with the Gospel" (20).

Then Pope John Paul II, both in his writing and in his extensive preaching throughout the world, repeatedly referred to a *new evangelization*. Anticipating the five hundred years of evangelization in the Americas from 1492 to 1992, John Paul first used the term *new evangelization* in an address to the Latin American Bishops in Port-au-Prince, Haiti, in 1983: "The commemoration of the half millennium of evangelization will gain its full energy if it is a commitment, not to re-evangelize but to a New Evangelization, new in its ardor, methods and expression."[6]

Earlier, in 1979, at Santo Domingo in the Dominican Republic, on the same island of Hispaniola, Pope John Paul preached on the history of evangelization in the Americas:

> This Dominican land was once the first to receive, and then to give impetus to, a grand enterprise of evangelization . . . laying the foundations of the heritage, become life, that we contemplate today in what was called the New World.
>
> From the first moments of the discovery, there appears the concern of the Church to make the kingdom of God present in the heart of the new peoples, races, and cultures; . . . the Church in this island was the first to demand justice and to promote the [defense] of human rights in the lands that were opening to evangelization.
>
> Lessons of humanism, spirituality and effort to raise man's dignity are taught to us by Antonio Montesinos, Córdoba, Bartolomé de las Casas, . . . and so many others. . . . The first International Law has its origin here with Francisco de Vitoria.
>
> The fact is that the proclamation of the Gospel and human advancement cannot be dissociated—this is the great lesson, valid also today. . . . The Church, an expert in humanity, faithful to the signs of the times, and in obedience to the pressing call of the last Council, wishes to continue today her mission of faith and [defense] of human rights. She calls upon Christians to commit themselves to the construction of a more just, human, and habitable world, which is not shut up within itself, but opens to God. (2-3)[7]

Later in 1990, Pope John Paul opened his encyclical letter *On the Permanent Validity of the Church's Missionary Apostolate* by saying:

> The mission of Christ the Redeemer, which is entrusted to the Church, is still very far from completion. As the second millennium after Christ's coming draws to an end, an overall view of the human race shows that this mission is still only beginning and that we must commit ourselves wholeheartedly to its service. It is the Spirit who impels us to proclaim the great works of God: "For if I preach the Gospel, that gives me no ground for boasting. For necessity is laid upon me. Woe to me if I do not preach the Gospel!" (1 Cor 9:16)
>
> In the name of the whole Church, I sense an urgent duty to repeat this cry of St. Paul. From the beginning of my Pontificate I have chosen to travel to the ends of the earth in order to show this missionary concern. My direct contact with peoples who do not know Christ has convinced me even more of the urgency of missionary activity, a subject to which I am devoting the present encyclical.
>
> The Second Vatican Council sought to renew the Church's life and activity in the light of the needs of the contemporary world. The Council emphasized the Church's "missionary nature," basing it in a dynamic way on the Trinitarian mission itself. The missionary thrust therefore belongs to the very nature of the Christian life. (1)[8]

Pope John Paul II went on to emphasize: "People today put more trust in witnesses than in teachers, in experience than in teaching, and in life and action than in theories. The witness of a Christian life is the first and irreplaceable form of mission: Christ, whose mission we continue, is the 'witness' par excellence (Rev 1:5; 3:14) and the model of all Christian witness" (42).

In this great tradition of evangelization and the defense of human rights, Pope Francis in 2013 opened the long introduction to his apostolic exhortation *Evangelii Gaudium* by saying:

The joy of the Gospel fills the hearts and lives of all who
encounter Jesus. Those who accept this offer of salvation are set free from sin, sorrow, inner emptiness and
loneliness. With Christ joy is constantly born new. In this
Exhortation I wish to encourage the Christian faithful to
embark upon a new chapter of evangelization marked by
this joy, while pointing out new paths for the Church's
journey in years to come. (1)

Pope Francis, later in the introduction, says, "Every form of
authentic evangelization is always 'new'. . . . The real newness
is the newness which God himself mysteriously brings about
and inspires, provokes, guides and accompanies in a thousand
ways" (11–12).

Pope Francis's impassioned call in chapters 1 and 2 of *The
Joy of the Gospel* for the transformation of the church's self-
understanding according a "missionary option" on the part
of all believers is further explored in chapter 4 on "The Social
Dimension of Evangelization." Pope Francis opens the chapter
saying: "To evangelize is to make the kingdom of God present
in the world. . . . I would now like to share my concerns about
the social dimension of evangelization, precisely because if this
dimension is not properly brought out, there is a constant risk
of distorting the authentic and integral meaning of the mission
of the evangelization" (176).

In the chapter's opening section on "Communal and societal
repercussions of the kerygma," Pope Francis speaks to the core
message of the Gospel: "The kerygma has a clear social con-
tent: at the very heart of the Gospel is life in community and
engagement with others" (177). In the next section on "The
kingdom and its challenge," Pope Francis writes:

The gospel is not merely about our personal relationship
with God. Nor should our love in response to God be seen
simply as an accumulation of small personal gestures to
individuals in need, a kind of "charity à la carte," or a
series of acts aimed solely at easing our conscience. The
gospel is about the kingdom of God (cf. Lk 4:43); it is

> about loving God who reigns in our world. To the extent
> that he reigns within us, the life of society will be a setting
> for universal fraternity, justice, peace and dignity. Both
> Christian preaching and life, then, are meant to have an
> impact on society. We are seeking God's kingdom. (180)

Saying of the Gospel, "Nothing human can be alien to it"
(182), Pope Francis undertakes in the remaining four sections
of chapter 4 on "The Social Dimension of Evangelization" to
do social analysis and engage the church in theological reflection on two pressing social questions, quoting Pope Benedict's
encyclical *Deus Caritas Est* (2005) to say, "If indeed 'the just
ordering of society and of the state is a central responsibility
of politics,' the Church 'cannot and must not remain on the
sidelines in the fight for justice'" (183). These two great issues
that Pope Francis says "strike me as fundamental at this time in
history" (185) are treated at length in the next two sections of
this chapter 4: "The inclusion of the poor in society" and "The
common good and peace in society." In the final and fourth section of this chapter, the pope briefly points to several additional
matters of importance in a consideration of "Social dialogue
as a contribution to peace": the dialogue between faith, reason, and culture; ecumenical dialogue; relations with Judaism;
interreligious dialogue; and social dialogue in a context of religious freedom. Pope Francis concludes the chapter by saying:
"Starting from certain social issues of great importance for the
future of humanity, I have tried to make explicit once again
the inescapable social dimension of the Gospel message and
to encourage all Christians to demonstrate it by their words,
attitudes and deeds" (258).

In chapters 1 and 5 of *Evangelii Gaudium*, Pope Francis
refers to the loftiness of our universal vocation as evangelists in
terms of a call to compassion. In chapter 1 on "The Church's
Missionary Transformation," Francis writes:

> Here I repeat for the entire Church what I have often said
> to the priests and laity of Buenos Aires: I prefer a Church
> which is bruised, hurting and dirty because it has been out

on the streets, rather than a Church which is unhealthy from being confined and from clinging to its own security. I do not want a Church concerned with being at the center and which then ends being caught up in a web of obsessions and procedures. If something should greatly disturb us and trouble our consciences, it is the fact that so many of our brothers and sisters are living without the strength, light and consolation born of friendship with Jesus Christ, without a community of faith to support them, without meaning and a goal in life. More than by fear of going astray, my hope is that we will be moved by the fear of remaining shut up within structures which give us a full sense of security, within rules which make us harsh judges, within habits which make us feel safe, while at our door people are starving and Jesus does not tire of saying to us: "give them something to eat" (Mk 6:37). (49)

And early in chapter 5 on "Spirit-filled Evangelizers"—and in chiastic relation to what we have heard just now in chapter 1 on "The Church's Missionary Transformation"—the pope writes that "we must reject the temptation to offer a privatized and individualized spirituality which ill accords with the demands of charity, to say nothing of the implications of the incarnation" (262). Christian spirituality, rather, involves a call to engagement:

Sometimes we are tempted to be that kind of Christian who keeps the Lord's wounds at arm's length. Yet Jesus wants us to touch human misery, to touch the suffering flesh of others. He hopes that we will stop looking for those personal or communal niches which shelter us from the maelstrom of human misfortune and instead enter into the reality of other people's lives and know the power of tenderness. Whenever we do so, our lives become wonderfully complicated and we experience intensely what it is to be a people, to be part of a people. . . . Jesus does not want us to be grandees who look down upon others, but men and women of the people. This is not an idea of the Pope, or one pastoral option among others; they are injunctions contained in the word of God which are so

clear, direct and convincing that they need no interpreta-
tions which might diminish their power to challenge us.
Let us live them *sine glossa,* without commentaries. By
so doing we will know the missionary joy of sharing life
with God's faithful people as we strive to light a fire in
the heart of the world. (270–271)

According to the Signs of the Times

In the late nineteenth century, as the United States recovered
from its bloodiest war, Europe was engaged in a class struggle.
Feudal Europe had given way to both the nation state and an
industrial economy. Karl Marx, in *The Communist Manifesto*,
called for a socialist economy to eliminate private ownership
and thus resolve the struggle between the impoverished working class and propertied owners of industrial capital.

In this rising tide of late nineteenth-century European so-
cialism, the Roman Catholic Church made its response in the
person of Pope Leo XIII. Leo wrote his encyclical letter on the
condition of human work (*Rerum Novarum*, 1891) in response
to *The Communist Manifesto*. Seventy years later, Pope John
XXIII, in his encyclical on Christianity and social progress
(*Mater et Magistra*, 1961), reaffirmed the opinion of his prede-
cessor Pope Pius XI in 1931 that *Rerum Novarum* was the
Magna Carta of the economic and social reconstruction of
the modern era.

One of the most significant aspects of Catholic Social
Teaching is the distinct methodological shift from classical
consciousness in the earlier documents to historical-contextual
consciousness in the later documents. Earlier documents began
with a statement of principles from natural law and then deduced a Christian social ethic from these first principles. *Rerum
Novarum*, for example, took as its starting point in natural law
the individual right to private property in order to fulfill the
responsibility of providing for one's family. It then deduced
that these rights and responsibilities of the individual and the
family take precedence in the social order over the rights of

the state. The encyclical therefore concluded that the Marxist impulse to alienate private property to state ownership is not to be supported.

Later documents—*Quadragesimo Anno* (On Restructuring the Social Order, Pius XI, 1931), *Mater et Magistra* (Christianity and Social Progress, John XXIII, 1961) and *Pacem in Terris* (Peace on Earth, John XXIII, 1963)—continue to deduce a Catholic social ethics from first principles in the natural law. In *Pacem in Terris*, however, the first indication could be seen of a methodological shift. Whereas John XXIII's methodology was classical and deductive in the main, he concluded each section of this encyclical with a short reflection on the signs of the times. Two years later, each section of *Gaudium et Spes,* the Vatican II Pastoral Constitution in the Modern World (1965), began with the signs of the times. This shift from natural law to signs of the times as the starting point for articulating a reflection on Catholic social ethics led to a more tentative and contextual form of expression in later documents. For example, on the eightieth anniversary of *Rerum Novarum* in 1971, Paul VI wrote in *Octogesima Adveniens*: "In the face of such widely varying situations, it is difficult for us to utter a unified message and to put forward a solution which has universal validity. Such is not our ambition, nor is it our mission. It is up to the Christian communities themselves to analyze with objectivity the situation which is proper to their own country, to shed on it the light of the principles of reflection, norms of judgment, and directives for action from the social teaching of the Church" (4).[9]

The whole of Catholic Social Teaching turns on its core principle of the dignity of the human person. Another development from earlier to later documents in the corpus can be traced in terms of an increasing emphasis on the freedom and quality of persons and their participation in society. The twentieth-century church responded to the challenge of totalitarianism with a defense of the freedom and dignity of the human person. In *Mater et Magistra*, John XXIII framed the ideal social order on the natural law values of truth, justice, and love. *Pacem in Terris* concretized a social order of truth, justice, charity, and freedom with the promulgation of a bill of human rights. The Second Vatican Council took the remarkable step of endorsing religious freedom. Paul VI introduced the expression *preferential respect due to the poor* in *Octogesima Adveniens* (23). An emphasis on participation was further endorsed by Pope John Paul II with his emphatic use of the word *solidarity* in *Sollicitudo Rei Socialis* (On Social Concern, 1987).

The documents of Catholic Social Teaching have repeatedly spoken for over one hundred years of the depersonalizing and dehumanizing effects of economic ideology as *slavery*. Catholic Social Teaching truly can be said to be documenting an era, an era of 125 years, in which workers, classes, and nations strain for economic and political inclusion. We live in an era of conversion—from slavery to solidarity.

The very life of John Paul II, of course, was closely aligned to the idea of Poland's solidarity movement. It is very interesting, however, that in his later encyclicals—*Veritatis Splendor* (The Splendor of Truth, 1993) and *Fides et Ratio* (Faith and Reason, 1998)—he seemed significantly to shift course as he cautioned against the steady movement since the 1960s toward historical consciousness and toward dialogue with the signs of the times in culture. In *Fides et Ratio*, he wrote:

> The word of God is not addressed to any one people or to any one period of history. Similarly, dogmatic statements, while reflecting at times the culture of the period in which they were defined, formulate an unchanging and ultimate truth. This prompts the question of how one can reconcile the absoluteness and the universality of truth with the unavoidable historical and cultural conditioning of the formulas which express that truth. The claims of historicism, I noted earlier, are untenable; but the use of a hermeneutic open to the appeal of metaphysics can show how it is possible to move from the historical and contingent circumstances in which the texts developed to the truth which they express, a truth transcending those circumstances. (95)[10]

This post-liberal or neo-orthodox allegiance resulted in public confusion over the meaning of the new evangelization and paradoxically may have contributed to several years of a more self-referential ecclesiastical focus on doctrine with a more doctrinaire understanding of preaching and catechesis, as well as a more defensive posture over and against culture.

Without discounting the church's rich natural-law tradition or its commitment to truth, Pope Francis seems urgently committed to reading the signs of the times as he considers and promotes the church's mandate to evangelization. In doing so, and in associating the word *evangelization* with a universal call to the faithful to be *missionary disciples* and *evangelists*, Francis has contributed clarity to the meaning of Paul VI's *evangelization of culture* and John Paul's *new evangelization*—a clarity and a call that have resonated with listeners throughout the world.

Pope Francis in Summary

Since the conclusion of Vatican II, synods of bishops from around the globe have convened thirteen times at the church's central see of Rome, with each synod teasing out a new dimension of the Vatican II message, and with successive popes issuing a series of post-synodal apostolic exhortations as ecclesial calls to Vatican II renewal and action.

As has been seen earlier in this manuscript, a number of these exhortations and synods have been pointedly relevant to the church's emerging understanding of its ministry of the Word today: *Evangelii Nuntiandi* (Evangelization in the Modern World, Paul VI, 1975), *Catechesi Tradendae* (Catechesis in Our Time, John Paul II, 1979), *Christifideles Laici* (The Vocation and Mission of the Lay Faithful in the Church and in the World, John Paul II, 1988), *Sacramentum Caritatis* (The Eucharist: Source and Summit of the Life and Mission of the Church, Benedict XVI, 2007), *Verbum Domini* (The Word of God in the Life and Mission of the Church, Benedict XVI, 2010), and most recently *Evangelii Gaudium* (The Proclamation of the Gospel in Today's World, also known as The Joy of the Gospel, Francis, 2013).

In preparation in 1987 for the synod of bishops on the subject of the vocation and mission of the laity, Pope John Paul II convened a consultation with laity. In one of several interventions at the conclusion of this consultation, Mr. Gabriel Ojo of Nigeria said to the pope:

> In various working groups we have been deliberating on the theme of the world meeting which is *A New Evangelization for the Building of a New Society.* We have reflected deeply on the two key concepts of the theme, namely new evangelization and new society. The emphasis of the new evangelization has been on the vocation and mission of laypeople in the church and in the world. The essential elements of the new evangelization include the total mobilization of all laypersons as bearers of the Good News and the discovery of the laypersons' personal Christian responsibility within the world which will make them become the leaven of the new society.[11]

Pope Francis could not have said these words better himself. It seems that in good measure the vitality of Francis's message is the manner in which his message represents a convergence of several essential themes of Vatican II: the church's engagement with the modern world as it reads the signs of the times, the sacramental authority of word and sacrament as summit and source in the church's liturgy, and the power of language and dialogue to mediate meaning in people's lives and in culture. Such mediation is made through the interpretive lenses of the Gospel and Catholic Social Teaching and also the baptismal rights and responsibilities of the laity as ambassadors of the Gospel.

In 2008, ecclesial attention turned to the Synod on the Word of God convened by Pope Benedict. His ensuing promulgation of *Verbum Domini* in 2010 successfully placed the Word of God and the ministry of the Word at the forefront of Catholic consciousness. In that document, as the scholar Benedict named the performative and sacramental nature of the Word in the church's life and ministry, the context was set perfectly for the church to receive a preacher as pope.

Thanks to his exceptional charism as a preacher, Pope Francis is showing us this performative character of the Word of God. On the one hand, Pope Francis is wonderfully gifted at telling us the Gospel in the context of our times—in his preaching, his interviews, and his writing. On the other hand, Pope Francis also demonstrates a remarkable talent at showing us the Gospel as he goes repeatedly to the peripheries—living in a hotel, driving a secondhand car, visiting prisons, and reaching out to celebrate the joys and touch the sufferings of real people.

If anything, Pope Francis's attention is not on himself; it is on us, his brothers and sisters in faith. In so many ways, he is showing and telling us to go and do likewise—to reach out to others, especially at life's peripheries, with the joy of the Gospel. In the spirit of Vatican II, and in the spirit of the resurrected Christ, Pope Francis has issued a call to action to all believers to be missionary disciples and evangelists.

An Easter Homily

Each year at his Easter Vigil homily, Pope Francis has held up Mary Magdalene both as the first disciple to testify to the resurrection and as a mirror for our own discipleship, testimony, and participation in the church's unbroken and ongoing mission of evangelization. Here, by way of sharing in Pope Francis's invitation into faith and mission, is Pope Francis's Easter Vigil homily at the Vatican Basilica on April 19, 2014:

> The Gospel of the resurrection of Jesus Christ begins with the journey of the women to the tomb at dawn on the day after the Sabbath. They go to the tomb to honor the body of the Lord, but they find it open and empty. A mighty angel says to them: "Do not be afraid!" (Mt 28:5) and orders them to go and tell the disciples: "He has been raised from the dead, and indeed he is going ahead of you to Galilee" (v. 7). The women quickly depart and on the way Jesus himself meets them and says: "Do not fear; go and tell my brothers to go to Galilee; there they will see me" (v. 10). "Do not be afraid," "do not fear":

these are words that encourage us to open our hearts to receive the message.

After the death of the Master, the disciples had scattered; their faith had been utterly shaken, everything seemed over, all their certainties had crumbled and their hopes had died. But now that message of the women, incredible as it was, came to them like a ray of light in the darkness. The news spread: Jesus is risen as he said. And then there was his command to go to Galilee; the women had heard it twice, first from the angel and then from Jesus himself: "Let them go to Galilee; there they will see me." "Do not fear" and "go to Galilee."

Galilee is the place where they were first called, where everything began! To return there, to return to the place where they were originally called. Jesus had walked along the shores of the lake as the fishermen were casting their nets. He had called them, and they left everything and followed him (cf. Mt 4:18-22).

To return to Galilee means to re-read everything on the basis of the cross and its victory, fearlessly: "do not be afraid." To re-read everything—Jesus' preaching, his miracles, the new community, the excitement and the defections, even the betrayal—to re-read everything starting from the end, which is a new beginning, from this supreme act of love.

For each of us, too, there is a "Galilee" at the origin of our journey with Jesus. "To go to Galilee" means something beautiful, it means rediscovering our baptism as a living fountainhead, drawing new energy from the sources of our faith and our Christian experience. To return to Galilee means above all to return to that blazing light with which God's grace touched me at the start of the journey. From that flame I can light a fire for today and every day, and bring heat and light to my brothers and sisters. That flame ignites a humble joy, a joy that sorrow and distress cannot dismay, a good, gentle joy.

In the life of every Christian, after baptism there is also another "Galilee," a more existential "Galilee": the experience of a personal encounter with Jesus Christ who called me to follow him and to share in his mission. In this sense, returning to Galilee means treasuring in my heart the living memory of that call, when Jesus passed my way, gazed at me with mercy and asked me to follow him. To return there means reviving the memory of that moment when his eyes met mine, the moment when he made me realize that he loved me.

Today, tonight, each of us can ask: What is my Galilee? I need to remind myself, to go back and remember. Where is my Galilee? Do I remember it? Have I forgotten it? Seek and you will find it! There the Lord is waiting for you. Have I gone off on roads and paths that made me forget it? Lord, help me: tell me what my Galilee is; for you know that I want to return there to encounter you and to let myself be embraced by your mercy. Do not be afraid, do not fear, return to Galilee!

The Gospel is very clear: we need to go back there, to see Jesus risen, and to become witnesses of his resurrection. This is not to go back in time; it is not a kind of nostalgia. It is returning to our first love, in order to receive the fire that Jesus has kindled in the world and to bring that fire to all people, to the very ends of the earth. Go back to Galilee, without fear!

"Galilee of the Gentiles" (Mt 4:15; Is 8:23)! Horizon of the Risen Lord, horizon of the Church; intense desire of encounter . . . Let us be on our way! [12]

5
A Testament of Devotion

> For all of you who were baptized into Christ have clothed yourselves with Christ. There is neither Jew nor Greek, there is neither slave nor free person, there is not male and female; for you are all one in Christ Jesus.

> —Galatians 3:27-28

What I Have Heard and Seen and Touched

I have taken pains in this short book to refrain from using the personal pronoun *I*, deferring to far more important voices in the church—the voices of the Second Vatican Council and its popes and especially, of course, Pope Francis. However, I do not wish to pretend that I have not heard and seen and been touched by these voices. Certainly in these chapters I have done my own theologizing in the hope of mediating theological meaning through a close reading of Pope Francis's message in ecclesial context. But I have been encouraged, also, to speak personally in this epilogue, for I too am a disciple and a preacher, and I too have been won over by Pope Francis. In the prologue, I asked preachers: what is your lifelong commitment, your practice, your labor of love, your preaching vocation? And I told preachers to be specific. Here I would like to do the same.

My parents grew up at one of the peripheries—my father Edwin in a hospital for crippled and indigent children and my mother June in a tuberculosis sanitarium. They were counseled not to have children, and it took effort to find a physician who would see a risky pregnancy through. My birth was induced six weeks early, and as it turns out my full-term birth date would have been the feast of Gregory Nazienzen, my patron—a preacher and theologian, a church administrator, a man with a gift for lifelong friendship, and a saint.

My father was Catholic, my mother (until she became Catholic) a Presbyterian—and though I was required to attend Sunday Mass and go to Wednesday evening religious education classes, as a child I was resistant to religion. Then one Wednesday evening when I was sixteen, I overheard our young priest, Fr. Paul Schumacher, say that Jesus had been raised from the dead. Though I had never willingly spoken to a priest, I went to him and apologized for not listening. I said, "I'm sorry, but I thought I heard you say that Jesus rose from the dead." He said, "Yes, Greg, I did say that."

All I can say is that in that short sentence, the Gospel was announced to me, and I heard and believed. Faith comes through hearing.

Faith also comes through seeing. It would be quite some time before I would be literate in my Christianity: for example, it is only by looking back now that I realize Fr. Paul announced the Resurrection to me during the Easter season. But I did see things differently. I saw the cross, and I would quietly walk the few blocks to the outdoor way of the cross in my rural community. I saw the Mass, and I went willingly and sometimes without telling others I was doing so. And I saw the priest, and I wanted what I saw. In the space of one sentence this heathen Catholic became a Christian believer—and in that same sentence a believer with a call to priesthood. I was shaped, I suppose, by my perceptions and my context, and today I would call my conversation most fundamentally a call to discipleship and only then a call to ecclesial ministry. And that being said, in my lifelong journey of discipleship I am an ordained presbyter today—going on forty years.

My seeing and hearing continued at St. John's University in Collegeville, Minnesota, where my father and his father had gone to school. I share the middle name John with my father, and St. John the Baptist is our shared patron: to this day I remain proud to call St. John's Abbey and University my spiritual home.

Like my father, I was a mathematics student. Though I attended daily Mass at St. John's and was being formed as a disciple by all I was hearing and seeing, I did not want to carry the brand of being a seminarian. I carried my call to priesthood quietly in my heart. During those years, I considered the diocesan priesthood and then was drawn to the Benedictines. And when I was age twenty-one, it was the Benedictines who generously discerned that I was called to preach. They referred me, therefore, to the Order of Preachers (also known as the Dominicans—after their thirteenth-century founder, St. Dominic Guzman). I was handed the phone number of the Dominican vocation director and told that he was expecting my call.

From the first time I hitchhiked to the Dominican novitiate in Winona, Minnesota, I was taken up in a love story. I entered religious life in 1969, when so many others all around me were leaving it. Certainly I was naive in terms of all the Vatican II upheaval in religious life, but I was truly in love, and I persisted.

Late in my theological studies for priesthood I undertook an eighteen-month internship at Catholic Campus Parish in Brookings, South Dakota—during which I was scheduled to take solemn vows and to be ordained a deacon. These decisions were easy enough in themselves, but when I tried to name for myself the Dominican charism, I remained perplexed.

Catholic Campus Parish had a mission church, a white frame building with a small congregation in White, South Dakota. There, for over a year, I preached every Saturday at their five o'clock Mass. Having been a student brother during the early years of Vatican II implementation, I must confess that I as a Dominican had never had a preaching class. But the Benedictines had sent me to the Dominicans to become a preacher, and now in White, South Dakota, I became one. As I became smitten by preaching, preaching and its preparation became a way of life. I eagerly gave about twenty hours a week to the task, often on long walks as I puzzled out my sermon. In South Dakota, the charism of the Order of Preachers revealed itself to me in practice.

While I had an excellent theological education at Aquinas Institute of Theology, that then was in Dubuque, Iowa, the only tangible evidence I have of those five years today is a valuable three-ring binder of typed church history notes. After graduate school, I still had so much to learn by way of practice.

A few years after ordination, I became active as the priest on the pastoral team of the St. Giles Community, a progressive Vatican II community of young families in Oak Park, Illinois. As I worked for the first time with lay colleagues who knew more theology and had vastly more pastoral experience than I, I was challenged to unlearn a lot of what I thought I knew as a graduate student—which is a way of saying I was challenged and given numerous uncomfortable opportunities to become a reflective practitioner.

In the course of becoming a reflective practitioner, I began to appreciate what it means not only to hear and see but also to touch Christ. As I continue to learn what this means—to touch Christ—I think it has to do with being brought by life to the foot of the cross and with encountering the risen Christ in the person-to-person transforming experience of touching his wounds in ourselves and in others. As a boy I took Thomas as my confirmation name, and in the human and cosmic experience of suffering, this sainted doubting believer, who with a heart close to cracking was invited to touch Jesus in his resurrection, also is my patron and twin.

Life brings every disciple to the foot of the cross. Suffering—both necessary and unnecessary—is a teacher, and I think a necessary doorway to reflective practice as a Christian. For me, it was only after I had put in the metaphorical ten thousand hours at discipleship and as I let go of naive and narrow preconceptions that I began more consciously to take counsel about my own suffering and to became a reflective practitioner, in my life and my ministry. Over a period of a few years, and with lots of communal help, I peeled away the duct tape that seemed to be holding my fragmenting first adult life structure together. At age thirty-four, I put my life back together again—still a Dominican, still a priest, and still in Christ for the long haul.

The long haul took me for nine years to Dominican Chapel Marywood in Grand Rapids, Michigan, where I preached and learned from the Grand Rapids Dominican Sisters how to be a civic religious leader and during which I pursued a Doctor of Ministry in preaching at Western Theological Seminary in Holland, Michigan. As it turned out, that degree positioned me as a reluctant forty-six-year-old to become a new director of field education and teacher of preaching at Aquinas Institute of Theology in St. Louis.

In that first year, I was startled to realize I liked teaching. And now twenty years later, I have joined the ten-thousand-hours club in several life-changing practices: preaching, living in community, friendship, teaching, and higher-education administration. I can look back and say that these practices have been the story of my Christian life, a story of faith and cross-and-resurrection discipleship.

The people I admire the most are those disciples who have gone to the foot of the cross and not looked back. Many of these have gone ahead of me in death, and they too are my patrons with many names. This growing crowd of witnesses—living, reborn in discipleship, and yet again reborn at the foot of the cross—are the people I love and with whom I already call it my privilege to spend eternity.

Communities of the Word

I believe in the formative power of conversation, and it seems my life of discipleship has turned on a handful of brief conversations—with my catechist when I was sixteen, with the Benedictine who referred me to the Dominicans when I was twenty, and—during a most difficult year when I was thirty-four—with the master of the order Damian Byrne, with two Dominican sister friends, and with the vicar provincial of my province—to each of whom I poured out my heart and from whom, each in their own way, I received the freedom to continue on the way of Dominican discipleship.

I remember when I was twenty-three taking a two-week summer course in the letters of St. Paul at Edgewood College in Madison, Wisconsin, from Jerome Murphy-O'Connor, a renowned Dominican from the *École Biblique* in Jerusalem. He told us that the most essential insight of St. Paul was that the practice of Christian life requires community—and that if we don't have community we need to find it, and that if we can't find it, we need to create it. In one perspective, my life of discipleship in community can be distilled to a number of life-transforming and life-saving, one-on-one conversations. From the perspective of the long haul, my discipleship also has played out in the ten-thousand-hour cumulation of prolonged God-given conversation with a few close friends and a very intuitive spiritual director.

Never in my life have I lived alone. Whether at home with family, in a college dormitory, or in Dominican houses, I always have lived in one after another community of disciples. The day-to-day communities that I have called home have been the place of domestic responsibility and more or less the safe place where brothers come home at the end of the day—tired, vulnerable, sometimes at their worst, and sometimes at their very best. Home is a place where discipleship plays out at perhaps its most mundane and day-in, day-out manner.

And then there is ministerial community, that also is a school of discipleship and that always seems to take me to the peripheries in unexpected ways. In my twenties, over a sequence of nine summers at Camp Tamarack in Upper Michigan, I learned with other young volunteers how to build community and share responsibility, how to reflect together on Scripture, and how to love one another in Christ. In my thirties and early forties at St. Giles Parish and then the Marywood motherhouse, I became immersed in the ministries of catechesis and adult formation. I was mentored in what it means to work with ministerial colleagues, and I enjoyed the privilege and challenge of preaching to worshipping communities of intentional disciples. And in my fifties and now sixties, I have grappled with what it means to be a teacher, an administrator, and a leader in a Dominican school teaching and forming men and women disciples on both the inbound track and the advanced track of ecclesial ministry and service.

During these most recent years, I also have been privileged to preach in two urban parishes and at a maximum security prison. When I moved to Missouri, I knew it was a death penalty state, but little did I know the ways in which this fact would take me to the periphery—to execution vigil services and ultimately at the invitation of one of my students to the prison itself. There in the course of annual Lenten days of prayer, I have met a core group of twenty or so Catholic offenders, in most cases condemned to life without parole or to death. These men study the Scriptures and companion one another in faith, they sponsor one another for the sacraments of initiation, they nurse and accompany the sick and dying in a hospice program of their own making, and they worship together in communion services or the Eucharist and on days of prayer. In this microcosm of church, the ministry of the Word plays out in catechesis, pastoral care, social service, and liturgical worship. Here at the periphery I have found brothers in Christ with a Pauline instinct for Gospel Actualized Community.

From where I hear and see and touch it, Christian community hangs on reflective conversation and testimony, study and reflection, accompaniment in suffering, and preaching and sacrament. We experience and live out our discipleship in friendship, in community, and in solidarity at the peripheries. Jerome Murphy-O'Connor was right: we need one another, and we need community as home base for being missionary disciples and evangelists. In the end, of course, God in Christ creates the beloved community, and God calls us all as friends and disciples. All this depends and thrives upon the constitutive and performative power of words and of the Word. Life in relationship and community is a prolonged conversation, a person-to-person transforming encounter of heart and mind and soul—making community and becoming our authentic selves in the Christian acts of hearing and seeing, speaking and showing, touching and serving.

My Preaching Life

My formative years as a college student at St. John's took place during the Vietnam War. My roommate Steven Kaster was a dear friend, and we had many conversations. Steve died in the war on the feast of All Souls just a few months after our graduation, and his funeral in the St. John's Abbey Church was my first preaching. I was a Dominican novice at the time.

It wasn't for another five years, working on my homilies while walking across the South Dakota State campus to the dairy school for peach ice cream, that I discovered the preaching gene in my Christian DNA. The Benedictines had seen this in me, but I needed to discover it and work it out for myself, day by day and week by week—this ecclesial charism and constitutive practice of Dominican life and mission.

Those were the days when folks were talking about preaching in terms of telling a story. I already had been a camp storyteller, but now I was telling a story by way of working out my own identity as a young Christian adult and by way of making a human connection to the students and farmers to whom I preached. By the grace of God, they found meaning in my early preaching, an acknowledgment that encouraged me to stay the course in what I was realizing to be the preaching life.

The Preaching Life is the title of a book by Episcopalian priest and homiletician Barbara Brown Taylor. The Order of Preachers has its own expression—*Sacra Praedicatio* (The Sacred Preaching)—a moniker by which the earliest Dominican communities were known and also an acknowledgment by the Dominican Movement today that ours is a communal way of Christian life that preaches. Preaching can be the summit and source of a whole Word-centered way of life. The most authentic preachers understand this. Read, for example, Marilynne Robinson's novel *Gilead,* in which rural Iowa Congregationalist minister John Ames is an icon of the studious disciple for whom preaching is a consuming spiritual practice and a way of discipleship. *The Preaching Life* and *Gilead* would be two fine books for any preacher's library.

The pursuit of a ministerial doctorate in preaching seemed opportune at the time of my ministry in Michigan, about fifteen years into my preaching life. My thesis—"A Paradigm for Preaching Personal and Social Transformation"—studied paradigm change in science and theology, in Catholic Social Teaching, in the life of the preacher and the church, and in the remarkable corpus of work by St. Louis University professor of humanities Walter Ong, SJ, whom I was privileged to interview and later to know more personally. I also explored with great benefit the unpublished work of Princeton University professor of politics Dr. Manfred Halpern on "Transformation: Its Theory and Practice in Personal, Political, Historical and Sacred Being."

My thesis concluded with a quotation from Annie Dillard about chopping wood—that for me was a metaphor for how the preaching life is an act of discipleship directed to the peripheries:

> At first, in the good old days, I did not know how to split wood. I set a chunk of alder on the chopping block and harassed it, at enormous exertion, into tiny wedges that flew all over the sandflat and lost themselves. What I did was less like splitting wood than chopping flints. After a few whacks my alder chunk still stood serene and unmoved, its base untouched, its tip a thorn, and then I actually tried to turn the sorry thing over and balance it on its wee head while I tried to chop its feet off before it fell over. God save us . . .
>
> One night, while all this had been going on, I had a dream in which I was given to understand, by the powers that be, how to split wood. You aim, said the dream—of course!— at the chopping block. It is true. You aim at the chopping block, not at the wood; then you split the wood, instead of chipping it. You cannot do the job cleanly unless you treat the wood as the transparent means to an end, by aiming past it.[1]

We disciples must, as St. Paul puts it, aim for the prize (Phil 3:14).

American homiletics is a growing field with an important body of classic and relevant literature. I am startled now to see how my doctoral study made no reference whatever to that literature. Not until three years later in 1994, when I was a first-year preaching teacher under the mentorship of American Catholic homiletics pioneer Joan Delaplane, OP, did I begin to read and then to meet such homiletic giants as Fred Craddock, David Buttrick, Eugene Lowry, and so many others of that greatest generation. That first year as a teacher, I also audited the Doctor of Ministry in Preaching course on theology of preaching taught by Mary Catherine Hilkert, OP, who that year was completing her important contribution to Catholic homiletics— *Naming Grace: Preaching and the Sacramental Imagination.* For twenty years now, I have taught that same course and have had so much opportunity to mentor hundreds of preachers and to keep abreast of a compelling homiletic, scriptural, liturgical, historical, and theological literature pertinent to the preaching life. With my students in 2001, I published a book of essays on the theology of preaching—in which, in the introduction, I was working out the idea of the Gospel Actualized Community:

> The Catholic Church in the United States certainly has changed in the twenty years since the United States Bishops' Conference promulgated *Fulfilled in Your Hearing: The Homily in the Sunday Assembly.* As baptized disciples engage in full, conscious, and active participation in apostolic and ecclesial life and as the presbyterate is shaken on several fronts by a sense of radical diminishment, the ministry of the Word has diversified. Today's gospel-actualized community calls into play a panoply of ministries of the Word: *catechesis* in Christian formation, *paraclesis* (if I might be permitted to search for a word) in pastoral care, *evangelization of culture* (an expression of popes Paul VI and John Paul II) in action for justice, and of course, at the summit and source of ecclesial life, *homilia (homily)*—preaching in the liturgical assembly. As I say elsewhere, "The mission of the preacher, therefore, according to his or her ministerial position in the

community, is to attend to the gospel actualization of
the community—in its aspects of pastoral care, Christian
formation, action for justice, and worship."[2]

Another formative experience in my preaching life, during
my tenure as president of the Catholic Association of Teachers
of Homiletics (CATH), was the annual meeting at which we
as Catholic homileticians celebrated the thirtieth anniversary
of *Fulfilled in Your Hearing* with a daylong extended dialogue
in Saint Paul, Minnesota, with the two principle authors of
the document—William Skudlarek, OSB, and Fred Baumer.
For twenty years now, multiple additional opportunities have
been extended to me to promote and participate in such lively
conversations about preaching with men and women who
have made preaching their life—with students, with teachers
at CATH and ecumenically at the Academy of Homiletics, with
scholars and pastors at theological colloquia, with Dominican
men and women, and with preachers of many dioceses. Little
did I imagine my life going in this direction, but all of it—
the call to conversion and discipleship, the communal life, the
preaching, the study, the teaching, and the promoting—is my
story of the preaching life.

Why Pope Francis Speaks to Me

I recently spoke with an athlete and fifty-four-year-old sport
cyclist, a professional healer and bodyworker, and a person
of absolute integrity—someone with deep instinctive understanding of "practice" but with little understanding of things
Catholic. When she asked me to say more about Pope Francis,
I said that my heart is moved by his message, and as I searched
for words to convey that message, I said, "He is inviting everyone to be missionaries at the edge." She said, "I get that,"
and she immediately spoke about the challenge in her urban
neighborhood of getting through to the growing number of
frightening and disrespecting preteen boys on the street. She
spoke also about her cycling and bodywork. I said there are

ten thousand ways to be a missionary at the edge, and we wondered what a wonderful world it would be if we all did so. And isn't that what Francis is inviting us to do?

The next morning, *The New York Times* displayed a large photo of Pope Francis on the front page above the fold—he had wandered into the employee lunchroom at the Vatican where he had taken a tray and was talking with workers who appeared to be from housekeeping or maintenance.[3] At the Vatican, he's "the man"—but he never forgets that he is a missionary at the edge, and the whole of humanity is puzzling and pondering his witness.

Like daily preaching, these stories multiply from day to day and are soon forgotten. But, taken together, they convey absolute authenticity and a sense of being "in touch." Pope Francis touches the joys and sorrows and sufferings and beauty at the human peripheries of the divine.

Thanks to what we have heard and seen and touched in Christ, we know by faith and because of what we have heard and seen and touched that God shines through in our lives. Pope Francis comprehends this, and it seems the Holy Spirit has sent him to the papal periphery in order to mirror the Gospel authenticity and the truth of Christian practice to the world. As we look into that mirror, we are attracted by what we see. Just as I look into the mirror and increasingly see my father, so the world looks at *Papa Francisco* and wants to be a better place.

The fact is that each of us lives on or at the edge in so many ways. Thanks to the missionary disciples and evangelists in our lives, we come to see ourselves and our stories as paschal mystery, and we reorient ourselves and our lives toward the cross. We come to see the ten-thousand-hour practices of our lives' vocation and in the lives of others as God's vocabulary for proclaiming the beloved community, the *basileia* of God of which the Scriptures speak.

God has "created" himself into our image, male and female. The reason we go to the periphery is because God always and everywhere goes there first, in the act of creation, in the redemptive acts of Jesus Christ, and in our presence and redemptive action. This is the amazing story of God in creation and in the ten thousand people and things. In our joys and sufferings and actions, resurrection shines through. Jesus has risen from the dead, and—*Alleluia*—so do we.

Pope Francis knows this. He knows that our vocation as Christians is to go with faith to the ten thousand peripheries of death and resurrection. Paradoxically for Christians, the peripheries become the center-point and holy ground from which we live our lives. Pope Francis invites us to join him—to be and to announce the hope of God's loving presence there.

Questions for Discussion

Preachers

1. Identify one or two things that characterize the preaching style of Pope Francis. What kind of impact on real lives does Pope Francis's preaching have? (chap. 1)

2. Is there a life-giving relationship between your Sunday pulpit and your community's catechesis, pastoral care, and action for justice? What is needed in order to make a Gospel Actualized Community? (chap. 1)

3. How could Catholic Social Teaching more comprehensively inform your preaching? Be specific. (chap. 2)

4. In what ways do you see your people being sent in their lives to be missionary disciples and evangelists? How can your community's preaching, catechesis, pastoral care, and solidarity with the poor intentionally support that goal? (chap. 2)

5. Think and pray about what Pope Francis is saying about preaching in *The Joy of the Gospel*. What could you do in the next week and the next three months to be a more effective preacher? (chaps. 3 and 4)

6. How does your life concretely bear witness to living as a missionary disciple and evangelist at the peripheries? Identify or cull out your call to conversion. (chaps. 4 and 5)

7. Name your preaching vocation. Be specific. (chap. 5)

Disciples

1. What is a concrete story you can tell about how Pope Francis has made you want to be a better person? What did he say or do that makes you want to grow, to change? (chap. 1)

2. How are you an active participant in the church's ministry of the Word in your faith community? How do you proclaim Good News in your day-to-day mundane life at home, at work, and elsewhere? (chap. 2)

3. How do the principles of Catholic Social Teaching stretch your understanding of missionary discipleship and your baptismal call to be an evangelist? (chap. 2)

4. Reflect upon and talk through the idea of discipleship as presented in the diagram on page 30. (chap. 2)

5. How would you like to grow as a missionary disciple? (chap. 2)

6. How can a faith community support good preaching? (chaps. 3 and 4)

7. How do you envision the church going to the peripheries for the sake of the Gospel? (chap. 4)

8. In what life practices are you a member of the ten-thousand-hour club? How do these practices take you to the edge, and how do they open up for you the possibility and the vocation of being a missionary disciple? (chap. 5)

Notes

1 A Preacher as Pope, *pages* 1–15

1. The preaching of Pope Francis (and of the other popes) can be found at the Vatican website at http://www.vatican.va, listed according to year and date.

2. Pope Francis, *I Ask You to Pray for Me: Opening a Horizon of Hope* (Mahwah, NJ: Paulist Press, 2013), 66.

3. Sofia Cavalletti, *The Religious Potential of the Child: The Description of an Experience with Children from Ages Three to Six* (Mahwah, NJ: Paulist Press, 1983), 23.

4. Quoted in Paul Vallely, *Pope Francis: Untying the Knots* (London: Bloomsbury, 2013), 155.

5. Pope Francis, Post-Synodal Apostolic Exhortation on the Proclamation of the Gospel in Today's World (*Evangelii Gaudium*), 24 November 2013. Vatican documents are cited by paragraph or section numbers unless otherwise indicated.

6. The Daily Meditations of Pope Francis, posted by the Official Vatican Network, http://www.news.va/en/sites/reflections (also in Spanish, French, Italian, and Portuguese).

7. St. Augustine, *De Doctrina Christiana* IV.12.27, in *Teaching Christianity*, The Works of Saint Augustine: A Translation for the 21st Century I/11, trans. Edmund Hill (Hyde Park, NY: New City, 1996), 215–16.

8. Pope Francis, homily (Rome: St. Cyril of Alexandria, December 1, 2013 [First Sunday of Advent]).

9. Pope Francis, homily (Rome: St. Thomas the Apostle, February 16, 2014 [Sixth Sunday in Ordinary Time]).

10. Vallely, *Pope Francis: Untying the Knots,* 155.

11. Pope Francis, Mass for the Imposition of the Pallium and Bestowal of the Fisherman's Ring for the Beginning of the Petrine

Ministry of the Bishop of Rome (Rome: St. Peter's Square, March 19, 2013).

12. Pope Francis, homily for the Chrism Mass (Rome: Vatican Basilica, March 28, 2013 [Holy Thursday]).

13. Pope Francis, homily for the Easter Vigil (Rome: Vatican Basilica, March 30, 2013 [Holy Saturday]).

14. Pope Francis, homily for the Easter Vigil (Rome: Vatican Basilica, April 19, 2014 [Holy Saturday]).

15. Pope Francis, homily for Pentecost (Rome: Vatican Basilica, June 8, 2014).

16. Pope Francis, *Angelus* (Rome: St. Peter's Square, January 6, 2014 [Feast of the Epiphany]).

2 You Cannot Imprison the Word of the Lord,
pages 16–33

1. Pope Francis, Encyclical Letter on the Light of Faith (*Lumen Fidei*), June 29, 2013.

2. Second Vatican Council, Pastoral Constitution on the Church in the Modern Word (*Gaudium et Spes*), December 7, 1965.

3. James D. Whitehead and Evelyn Eaton Whitehead, *Method in Ministry: Theological Reflection and Christian Ministry,* rev. ed. (Kansas City, MO: Sheed & Ward, 1995).

4. Second Vatican Council, Constitution on the Sacred Liturgy (*Sacrosanctum Concilium*), December 4, 1963.

5. Ibid.

6. Pontifical Biblical Commission, "The Interpretation of the Bible in the Church," in *Origins* 23, no. 29 (January 6, 1994): 522. See section IV.C.1.

7. Bishops' Committee on Priestly Life and Ministry, *Fulfilled in Your Hearing: the Homily in the Sunday Assembly* (Washington, DC: United States Conference of Catholic Bishops, 1982). *FIYH* also is published as Appendix A in *Preaching in the Sunday Assembly: A Pastoral Commentary on* Fulfilled in Your Hearing, ed. James A. Wallace, CSsR (Collegeville, MN: Liturgical Press, 2010). Citations of *FIYH* are given using the paragraph numbers in the Liturgical Press appendix. See section on "The Homily and Faith" in chapter 3 of *Fulfilled in Your Hearing.*

8. Saint John Paul II, Post-Synodal Apostolic Exhortation on Catechesis in Our Time (*Catechesi Tradendae*), October 16, 1979.

9. Richard R.Gaillardetz, *Transforming Our Days: Spirituality, Community and Liturgy in a Technological Culture* (New York: Crossroad, 2000), 90.

10. Blessed Pope Paul VI, Apostolic Exhortation on Evangelization in the Modern World (*Evangelii Nuntiandi*), December 8, 1975—promulgated on the tenth anniversary of the closing of Vatican II.

3 The Gospel Preached with Unction, *pages* 34–45

1. Pope Francis, homily for the Chrism Mass (Rome: Vatican Basilica, March 28, 2013 [Holy Thursday]).

2. Trish Sullivan Vanni, "*Fulfilled in Your Hearing:* A Narrative History," appendix B in *Preaching in the Sunday Assembly: A Pastoral Commentary on* Fulfilled in Your Hearing, ed. James A. Wallace, CSsR (Collegeville, MN: Liturgical Press, 2010). Citations of *FIYH* are given using the paragraph numbers in the Liturgical Press appendix.

3. Second Vatican Council, Decree on the Ministry and Life of Priests (*Presbyterorum Ordinis*), December 7, 1965.

4. See section on "The Preacher as Mediator of Meaning" in chapter 1 of *Fulfilled in Your Hearing,* 12–15.

5. See section on "Homiletic Style" in chapter 3 of *Fulfilled in Your Hearing.*

6. Pope Francis, homily for the Chrism Mass (Rome: Vatican Basilica, March 28, 2013 [Holy Thursday]).

7. Pope Francis, Post-Synodal Apostolic Exhortation on the Proclamation of the Gospel in Today's World (*Evangelii Gaudium*), November 24, 2013.

8. United States Conference of Catholic Bishops, *Preaching the Mystery of Faith: The Sunday Homily* (Washington, DC: USCCB, 2013), http://www.usccb.org/beliefs-and-teachings/vocations/priesthood/priestly-life-and-ministry/upload/usccb-preaching-document.pdf. Chapters include "The Biblical Foundations for the Church's Preaching Ministry"; "The Ministry of Liturgical Preaching"; "The One Ordained to Preach"; "Interpreting the Scriptures and Preparing the Homily." Citations are given by page number.

9. Pope Benedict XVI, Post-Synodal Apostolic Exhortation on the Word of the Lord (*Verbum Domini*), September 30, 2010.

4 We Testify to the Word with Our Lives, *pages* 46–64

1. Pope Francis, Post-Synodal Apostolic Exhortation on the Proclamation of the Gospel in Today's World (*Evangelii Gaudium*), November 24, 2013.

2. *Code of Canon Law: Latin-English Edition, New English Translation* (Washington, DC: Canon Law Society of America, 2012).

3. Canon 767.1 has been interpreted variously by bishops in different dioceses according to pastoral need, and in relation to Canon 766 that says, "Lay persons can be permitted to preach in a church or oratory, if necessity requires it in certain circumstances or it seems advantageous [*utilitas*] in particular cases, according to the prescripts of the conference of bishops and without prejudice to can. 767, §1," and in relation to Canon 772.1 that says, "In the exercise of preaching . . . all are to observe the norms issued by the diocesan bishop." See also the "Promulgation on Implementing Canon 766 of the Code of Canon Law" (United States Conference of Catholic Bishops, 2002) and "*Redemptionis Sacramentum* on certain matters to be observed or to be avoided regarding the Most Holy Eucharist" (The Congregation for Divine Worship and the Discipline of the Eucharist, 2004).

4. See also the following canons:

225.1 Since, like all the Christian faithful, lay persons are designated for the apostolate through baptism and confirmation, they are bound by the general obligation and possess the right as individuals, or joined in associations, to work so that the divine message of salvation is made known and accepted by all persons everywhere in the world. This obligation is even more compelling in those circumstances in which only through them can people hear the gospel and know Christ.

225.2 According to each one's own condition, they are also bound by a particular duty to imbue and perfect the order of temporal affairs with the spirit of the gospel and thus to give witness to Christ, especially in carrying out these same affairs and in exercising secular functions.

759. By virtue of baptism and confirmation, lay members of the Christian faithful are witnesses of the gospel message by word and the example of a Christian life; they can also be called upon to cooperate with the bishop and presbyters in the exercise of the ministry of the word.

5. Blessed Pope Paul VI, Post-Synodal Apostolic Exhortation on Evangelization in the Modern World (*Evangelii Nuntiandi*), December 8, 1975.

6. Saint John Paul II, Opening Address of the Nineteenth General Assembly of CELAM, Port-au-Prince, Haiti, March 9, 1983, *L'Osservatore Romano* English Edition 16/780 (April 18, 1983), #9, as cited in part II of the Statement by the USCCB Committee on Evangelization and Catechesis, "Disciples Called to Witness: The New Evangelization" (Washington, DC: United States Conference of Catholic Bishops, 2012), http://www.usccb.org/beliefs-and-teachings /how-we-teach/new-evangelization/disciples-called-to-witness.

7. Saint John Paul II, Eucharistic Homily at Independence Square, Santo Domingo, Dominican Republic, January 25, 1979.

8. Saint John Paul II, Encyclical Letter on the Permanent Validity of the Church's Missionary Mandate (*Redemptoris Missio*), December 7, 1990.

9. Blessed Pope Paul VI, Apostolic Letter on the Eightieth Anniversary of *Rerum Novarum* (*Octogesima Adveniens*), May 14, 1971.

10. Saint John Paul II, Encyclical Letter on Faith and Reason (*Fides et Ratio*), September 14, 1998.

11. Pontifical Council for the Laity, *A New Evangelization for the Building of a New Society: World Consultation in View of the Synod of Bishops 1987* (Vatican City: Vatican Polyglot Press, 1987), 93.

12. Pope Francis, homily for the Easter Vigil (Rome: Vatican Basilica, March 30, 2013 [Holy Saturday]).

5 A Testament of Devotion, *pages 65–77*

1. Annie Dillard, *The Writing Life* (New York: Harper & Row, 1989), 42–43.

2. Gregory Heille, "Making the Scriptures Relevant," in *Theology of Preaching: Essays on Vision and Mission in the Pulpit*, ed. Gregory Heille (London: Melisende, 2001), 11, citing Gregory Heille, "The State of Catholic Preaching: What's Happening in the Pulpits of Our Parishes on Sunday and Is It What We Really Want?" *Seminary Journal* 5:3 (Winter 1999), 38–39.

3. "Ahem, Your Holiness? Please Pass the Salt," *The New York Times,* July 26, 2014; photo: L'Osservatore Romano, via Associated Press, http://www.nytimes.com/imagepages/2014/07/26/world/europe /POPE-copy.html.